SHEroes of the Bible

SHEROES
of the Bible

Lauren L. Nelson

NEW YORK

LONDON • NASHVILLE • MELBOURNE • VANCOUVER

SHEroes of the Bible

A Novel

Published in New York, New York, by Morgan James Publishing. Morgan James is a trademark of Morgan James, LLC. www.MorganJamesPublishing.com

Morgan James BOGO™

A **FREE** ebook edition is available for you or a friend with the purchase of this print book.

CLEARLY SIGN YOUR NAME ABOVE

Instructions to claim your free ebook edition:
1. Visit MorganJamesBOGO.com
2. Sign your name CLEARLY in the space above
3. Complete the form and submit a photo of this entire page
4. You or your friend can download the ebook to your preferred device

ISBN 9781631955570 paperback
ISBN 9781631955587 ebook
Library of Congress Control Number:
2021904057

Cover & Interior Design by:
Christopher Kirk
www.GFSstudio.com

Morgan James is a proud partner of Habitat for Humanity Peninsula and Greater Williamsburg. Partners in building since 2006.

Get involved today! Visit
MorganJamesPublishing.com/giving-back

TABLE OF CONTENTS

ACKNOWLEDGMENTS

"Oh Lord my God, You have performed many wonders for us. Your plans for us are too numerous to list. You have no equal. If I tried to recite all your wonderful deeds, I would never come to the end of them."

Psalm 40:5 (NLT)

Jesus, thank You for choosing me to share the lives of these amazing women from the Bible. I love following You—for there is so much adventure when I do! Thank You for setting me free from fear so that I can obey all that You ask me to do. Thank You that Your love will always be greater than my fears!

I owe an enormous debt of gratitude to the following people without whom I would have never completed this book:

To my editors, Arlyn Lawrence and Heather Sipes, with Inspira Literary Solutions, who beautifully shaped my book into what it is today. Thank you for believing in me and for introducing me to Morgan James Publishing, who gave this book wings to advance across the world.

To my sister, Kristin, whose refinement of my stories breathed life into them. Thank you for grasping hold of my vision from the very beginning and for spending so much time talking with me about, and wrestling with, how to share these incredible women's stories.

To my husband, Kyle, for helping me keep my perspective childlike and for encouraging me to continue writing when, at times, I wanted to quit. Thank you for your constant love and for always believing in me.

To my son, Noah, for giving the best hugs and for bringing me so much joy. Your name means "comfort" and you have certainly been that to me. I love you to the moon and back! I pray that when you grow older, you will choose to marry a woman who exemplifies all the qualities of a SHERo. I pray she will be strong, courageous, and that she will follow the Lord's lead no matter what comes her way.

And last, but not least, to my beautiful daughter, Kyah, whose innocent question was the reason I wrote this book. Thank you for being you! Your joy, laughter, and smiles bring such light to my life. "I love you a bushel and a peck!" May you be inspired by this book to continue to become the brave and strong SHERo that God created you to be! Your passion and love of worship is a weapon in the Lord's hand, and I'm excited to watch God do amazing things through you! Oh, and keep writing! I know in my heart that you will inspire the world with your words.

PREFACE

This book was written after a conversation I had with my then seven-year-old daughter, Kyah. We were on our way to church when she said, "Mom, I have a question…why are boys more important than girls?"

I was shocked! I said, "What do you mean?"

Then she said, "It just seems like God thinks boys are more important than girls because all we ever learn about in church are boys."

Her question ran through my head and heart for the next few days. I wanted Kyah to know her importance as a daughter of God and for her to know that He values girls and has a great plan for their lives, just as He does for boys. There are so many women mentioned throughout the Bible and I couldn't believe she had only heard of a couple. The Lord had a PERSONAL relationship with each of these women and He loved to watch them respond in faith and trust Him when He asked them to do something.

Over the next few weeks, I began to teach Kyah stories in the Bible about women who trusted God and did amazing things because of their love for Him. Kyah treasured hearing about the way these women lived. She begged me every night for another story. I couldn't write fast enough for her! Kyah wanted to be just like the women in the Bible. She wanted to be a SHERO—a girl who is a hero. She wanted to be brave and courageous and to live her life for God.

That is how "SHEROES of the Bible" came to be. I pray that as you read these words, you, too, will trust God with your life and know that He loves you. God has called you to be a mighty girl that trusts in His goodness and love—even in really tough situations.

Lauren

INTRODUCTION

God used many women in the Bible to do some pretty amazing things! We are going to take a journey with some SHEROES who experienced God in their lives in a significant way. My hope and prayer is that you understand that God still does incredible things today, and He wants to do them through you. God wants you to become a SHERO for Him!

What is a SHERO? Here are a few things that mark a SHERO:

Satisfied only in God—SHEROES want the Lord more than anything else in this world. They hunger and thirst for more of God, just like we hunger and thirst for food and water.

Heart to do what He asks—SHEROES find joy in doing what God asks them to do and they love to tell everyone what He has done for them.

Ears to hear Him speak—SHEROES listen to what God says in all situations.

Rescuer—SHEROES believe that God is their rescuer and they do not let fear stop them from helping rescue others.

Obedience—SHEROES let go of what they want so they can do what God says is best. They are brave and courageous as they trust God.

We are going to learn about some SHEROES who experienced hard stuff, but they chose to say yes to God and to trust Him to rescue and comfort them. At the end of this book, I hope your prayer will be, "God, you rescued those girls from some pretty scary situations. I know you can rescue me too!"

Let's give God all of our fears and ask Him to teach us to trust Him every day and every moment. Now, let's meet some SHEROES who lived a long, long time ago…

SHEROES
of the *Bible*

WOMEN OF THE
OLD TESTAMENT

SHIPHRAH AND PUAH

SHEroes of Exodus, Chapter 1

"... But because the midwives feared God, they refused to obey the King's orders..."

Exodus 1:17 (NLT)

"It's a boy!" shouted Shiphrah to her friend, Puah, and to the baby's mother. A precious new baby had just been born into the world! Shiphrah and Puah loved their jobs as midwives—helping babies be born safely and then taking care of the new mothers.

The baby's parents smiled at each other with happiness, but they exchanged worried looks, too. They were both excited and afraid at the same time.

The new parents, and the midwives, Shiphrah and Puah, were Hebrews. They lived in Egypt, the land of the pyramids. Although Egypt was not their home, the king of Egypt—called

"Pharaoh," liked the Hebrews so much that he gave them his best land to build their villages.

While they were living in Egypt, God blessed the Hebrews with so many children that it was hard to count them all. Each family had babies and then those babies grew up and had more babies. Before you knew it, the Hebrews were more numerous than the Egyptians!

During this time, the Pharaoh who had loved the Hebrew people died, and a new Pharaoh came into power. This new ruler became afraid that the Hebrews were growing too quickly in strength and numbers, and he thought to himself, "What if they take over Egypt? I have to make sure that doesn't happen!"

So, Pharaoh made the Hebrews his slaves, in order that they wouldn't get too powerful for the Egyptians. He made the Hebrews work hard day and night in the hot desert sun without being paid. They were forced to build the Egyptians' homes and kingdom. They had to make bricks out of the clay that covered the ground, and their taskmasters beat them if they didn't make enough. To make things worse, the Egyptians forced the Hebrew slaves to deliver the bricks on heavy carts that they had to push by hand. Doesn't that sound terrible?

Even though life was very hard for the Israelites, God continued to bless them with more and more children. The more they suffered, the more babies they had!

When it was time for the Hebrew mothers to give birth to their babies, they would call for special nurses called "midwives," who would come to their homes and help them. Shiphrah and Puah were the two lead nurses who oversaw all the other nurses in Egypt. They had a big job; they made sure that all the babies born were delivered healthy.

The Pharaoh continued to be fearful of how many Hebrew boys were being born. He wasn't worried about the girls, just the boys, because he thought the boys would grow up and form an army to fight against him. So he made a plan to get rid of all the Hebrew boy babies as soon as they were born. He called Shiphrah and Puah to his palace and commanded them, "Every time you help a Hebrew woman have a baby, if it's a boy, kill him, but if it's a girl, let her live. That way we can stop the Hebrews from taking over Egypt."

Shiphrah and Puah feared if they didn't do what the Pharaoh told them, he might kill them. But they loved God more than they feared the Pharaoh. Shiphrah and Puah knew that something must be done to stop this horrible order from taking place, and they knew that as the lead midwives, they were the only ones who could do anything about it. Shiphrah and Puah were about to follow God's plan and become SHEroes!

Shiphrah and Puah were in charge of many other midwives, so they gathered all who they knew loved God and told them the Pharaoh's terrible plan. All the women bravely agreed to save the Hebrew boy babies from being killed. They knew that every time they saved a baby boy, they were risking their own lives, but they couldn't stand by while innocent children were hurt!

This was their plan: each time a Hebrew woman gave birth to a baby, the nurses made sure to do all they could to help her deliver a healthy child—boy or girl. The mothers of the babies then risked punishment or even death by bravely hiding the baby boys from the Egyptians.

After a while, the Pharaoh ordered Shiphrah and Puah to come and see him at his palace. "Why are there still Hebrew boys being born?" he thundered.

They stood frozen in fear. Cleverly, they told him, "The Hebrew women are so strong that the babies are already born before we get there!" And the Pharaoh believed them.

Shiphrah and Puah, and many midwives and mothers, made the choice to trust God in spite of their fear of the Pharaoh. They saved countless lives, including a boy named Moses. God had an amazing plan to one day use Moses to rescue His people, the Hebrews, from slavery in Egypt and bring them to a beautiful new land—a land where they were free. Moses would lead the way for the greatest rescuer the world has ever known—Jesus!

Devotion

1. Shiphrah and Puah feared Pharaoh and his army, but they trusted God despite their fears. What are some things you are afraid of?

2. Take a moment to talk to God about your fears and ask Him to give you courage to trust that God is bigger than anything you are afraid of.

3. God often gives us friends or family to help us face our fears. Shiphrah and Puah faced their fears together. Who is someone you can face your fears with?

Jochebed, Miriam, and the Egyptian Princess

SHEroes of Exodus, Chapter 2

"... She saw that he was a special baby and kept him hidden for three months."

Exodus 2:2 (NLT)

Jochebed was scared. She was a Hebrew—and because of that, a slave of Egypt's cruel Pharaoh. The Pharaoh wanted her baby boy—and all the Hebrew boy babies—dead! He was afraid they might grow up and take over Egypt. Thanks to Shiphrah, Puah, and the rest of the midwives who helped save the newborn Hebrew boys, Jochebed's child—Moses—was still alive, but in hiding.

The Hebrews were continuing to grow strong, and this made the Pharaoh furious. He ordered his army to throw every Hebrew newborn boy into the Nile River so they wouldn't grow up and form an army and attack Egypt one day.

Jochebed couldn't let this happen to her precious baby. God had spoken to her heart and told her that there was something special about her son. So, she called on her daughter Miriam to help her, and together these two SHEROES made sure that Moses would live and fulfill God's plan for his life!

When Moses was three months old, his mother could no longer hide him because, like most babies, he would cry and make a lot of noise. She knew the Egyptians would soon find him and kill him. So, she prayed that God would help show her how to keep Moses safe.

Jochebed knew the only place her son could possibly escape the Pharaoh was in the very same river that the Pharaoh had ordered the babies to be thrown into—the Nile River. The river was dangerous, cold, and filled with crocodiles. But there was no other way to send her son to safety than to trust God and place him into a basket and float it on the Nile River.

She stood at the edge of the river, shaking in fear, as she prayed for protection for Moses. She gently placed him in a basket that would float and keep her precious boy from falling into the crocodile-filled waters. She was trusting the Lord would keep him safe.

Jochebed then asked her daughter Miriam to follow the basket as it floated along the river so she could make sure Moses was safe. Miriam was only ten years old. She knew if she was caught saving Moses, the Pharaoh would punish her. But she loved her baby brother, so she gathered up all of her courage and carefully hid among the tall reeds, hiding as best she could. Her heart filled with sadness as she listened to him softly cry while he floated down the river.

Miriam followed the basket for a long time, until she finally saw the basket drift toward the shore—right in front of the Pharaoh's palace! *Oh no,* Miriam thought. *This is the very person we are trying to keep Moses away from!* But suddenly, Miriam saw a beautiful princess, the daughter of Pharaoh, washing in the Nile River.

The princess heard the baby crying in the distance and looked over to the tall reeds at the water's edge. Then she saw it—a basket, just resting on the bank of the river. She curiously waded toward the basket and couldn't believe what she saw. There was a baby inside! She gasped, as she realized that this was one of Hebrew babies her father had ordered to be killed.

The princess was troubled as she looked at this sweet baby. She picked him up and held him close to her body. Her love moved her to action. In that very moment, she decided she was going to keep this child and raise him as her son. She named the baby Moses, which means "taken out of the water."

Quickly, she realized she didn't have anything

to feed this baby. He must be hungry! Miriam was still watching close by, and saw that the princess loved her brother. She bravely waded over to the princess. "Hello," Miriam said softly. "I can find a Hebrew woman who can feed him for you…" The princess was so relieved!

"Oh, yes," she said. "I will pay money to whomever you find that can feed my Moses."

With joy in her heart, Miriam ran as quickly as she could to find her mother. God had rescued her brother! She found her mother and shared the good news. "He is in good hands!" Miriam cried. "The princess of Egypt wants to raise him as her own and she needs YOU to feed him!"

Jochebed's heart was filled with joy. She was so thankful that God had saved her son, and that he would now be safe under the protection of the Princess of Egypt. Better yet, Jochebed now had the opportunity to care for, feed, and spend time with the son she had just given up!

Jochebed fed and cared for Moses for three years, helping him grow healthy and strong. However, when Moses was three years old, it was time for Jochebed to make the ultimate sacrifice. She returned her little boy to the palace so the princess could raise him as her own son. Even though Jochebed missed her son, she thanked God for His kindness and protection. She knew in her heart that God had saved Moses for something truly special!

Because these women—Jochebed, Miriam, and the Princess of Egypt—listened to God and trusted Him, God used Moses to rescue the Hebrews from slavery in Egypt. After many years, God would use him to part the Red Sea, and lead God's people through the desert to their Promised Land.

These SHEROES, through their faith and obedience, were an important part of God's special plan!

Devotion

1. Baby Moses was a precious gift to Jochebed and Miriam. As hard as it was to send Moses away, they trusted that God would take care of him. Have you ever trusted God with something that was precious to you?

2. God protected Moses by bringing him to the Pharaoh's palace and placing him under the protection of the Egyptian princess. God showed Jochebed and Miriam that they could trust Him. Is there a difficult situation in your life right now that you want to trust God with?

3. Sometimes it is difficult to see that your choices can impact other people's lives, for good or bad. Who is someone who has made a difference in your life for good, and why?

RAHAB

SHERo of Joshua, Chapters 2-6

"... For the Lord your God is the supreme God of the heavens above and the earth below."

Joshua 2:11 (NLT)

The Israelites—as the Hebrews were also called—were tired and discouraged. When Moses led them out of slavery in Egypt, God had promised them their own land—one that was "flowing with milk and honey." So, they waited for their Promised Land.

But to get to this Promised Land, they had to travel through a huge desert. This desert was harsh and uncomfortable. There was no milk and there certainly wasn't any honey. It had been forty years since they left Egypt. Many babies had been born and many old people had died, yet they still had not reached their Promised Land.

Throughout these forty years in the desert, God continued to provide for His people. He rained down food from the sky called manna, and He even provided water from a rock when they were thirsty! He told Moses to remind the Israelites they were His chosen people. "I chose you to be mine, not because of anything you have done, but because I love you," God said. Comforted by His love, they continued to march forward in search of their Promised Land.

Finally, in their fortieth year in the desert, the Israelites came to the edge of a land called Canaan. Canaan was beautiful and unlike anything the Israelites had ever seen! This land was spacious and green with many large fruit trees. The Jordan River was nearby and provided cool, fresh water to drink. Honey dripped from hives like liquid gold and countless cattle provided sweet, creamy milk. The Israelites could hardly believe what they saw.

There was only one problem…the land of Canaan was already taken. A group of wicked people, called the Canaanites, lived there. They worshipped false gods and did horrible things.

Although the Israelites were afraid, Moses' helper, Joshua, was brave. He was willing to do whatever God asked him to do, no matter how scared he was. God gave Joshua an idea. *What if he sent two spies into Canaan to learn how they could take the land?*

Canaan had one main city, the city of Jericho. Joshua found two brave men who were willing to complete this mission and explore the land. They needed to find out about the city's water supply, how much food was there, and learn more about Jericho's army.

The spies were amazed by how large and how grand the city was! It was encircled by two huge walls. On top of the walls were four towers, where Jericho's army stood watch for invaders.

The spies slipped through the main gates, pretending to be travelers from a distant land. Once inside, the spies could see that the city was well supplied with food—and there was even a river that ran through the city—supplying it with fresh water.

The Israelites had hoped to circle the city of Jericho and trap the Canaanite people inside until they ran out of food and water. But the spies could see that it would take months for the Canaanites to run out of supplies! The spies were discouraged. They knew the Lord had promised them the land, but their faith was shaken as they looked at all the problems they would have to overcome.

The spies decided to visit one of the homes located inside the outer wall, so they could easily escape if they needed to. There, they met Rahab, who ran a business for foreign travelers visiting Jericho.

While the spies spoke with Rahab, someone recognized them as spies, and they immediately told the King of Canaan. "The Israelites are here!" they exclaimed. "They are going to attack us for our land!" they told him.

Furious, the King sent men to Rahab's home. They pounded on the door and shook the whole house. "Bring out the men who visited you! They have come to spy on our land!" they shouted.

The Israelite spies stood there, frozen. They knew they would be killed if they were caught. But Rahab acted quickly, and she led the spies to the top of her roof where she was drying strips of cloth. She told the men to hide in the piles. "Shhhhhh" she told them, as she backed away to talk to the King's men.

Rahab took a deep breath and bravely opened the door. "Yes, I spoke to them," she said to the soldiers. "But I didn't know where they were from. They left a little while ago. If you hurry, you might catch them!" The King's men left quickly in the direction Rahab pointed.

Rahab quietly returned to her roof and spoke to the spies. "I know that the Lord has given you this land," she said. "Panic has fallen on our city because we have heard how the Lord parted the Red Sea for your people." Then, she lifted her hands toward the sky and said, "The Lord your God, He is the true God of heaven and earth!" The spies were amazed to find a believer in God among the Canaanites, and that God had led them straight to her!

Before they left, Rahab asked them one last question. "When you capture this city, will you please take care of me and my family?" The spies promised that if she helped them escape— and didn't tell anyone of their plan—they would protect her. Quickly and quietly, she helped the men escape out a window and used a rope to lower them to the ground outside of the city wall. Once their feet hit the ground, they ran as fast as they could to escape the King's men.

The spies returned to the Israelites with the exciting news: "The people of Jericho are terrified because of all that God has done for Israel. This is going to be our land!"

That night, the Lord spoke to Joshua. "You must march around the city of Jericho for six days," He said. "On the seventh day, you will blow your trumpet, and those huge walls of Jericho will tumble to the ground." These certainly seemed like funny instructions, but Joshua and the Israelites obeyed.

On the seventh day of marching, when the Israelites blew their trumpets, the walls of Jericho tumbled to the ground in a cloud of dust and the Canaanites were driven out. Miraculously, the portion of the wall where Rahab lived did not fall down and she and her family were rescued.

Because of Rahab's faith and obedience, the Israelites invited her to become part of their family. This SHERo chose to believe God and trust His plan, even when no one else in Jericho did. And, not only did Rahab's bravery help lead God's people into their Promised Land, but she also eventually became the great, great (many greats!) grandmother of God's Promised Rescuer—Jesus!

Devotion

1. Rahab heard about all that God had done for the Israelites, and so chose to believe in Him. What are some things you have heard about God, whether from the Bible or other people's lives, that help you believe in Him?

2. God invited the Israelites into His family, and then they invited Rahab into their family. There are many different types of families. Some families we are born into and some we join later. What does it mean to you to be part of a family?

3. Do you want to be part of God's family, just like Rahab? If so, just tell God that you want to be part of His family. He will be SO excited you asked! God loves having a BIG family. In His family, everyone is welcome!

DEBORAH AND JAEL

SHEROES of Judges, Chapters 4-5

"... Get ready! This is the day the Lord will give you victory over Sisera, for the Lord is marching ahead of you!"

Judges 4:14 (NLT)

The Israelites were discouraged, sad, and mad at themselves. They were slaves . . . again. After finally arriving in the Promised Land, they had made some very bad choices. They had defeated the wicked people of Canaan, but then began to worship the Canaanites' false god. Big mistake.

They'd learned the truth the hard way. The Canaanites' god was NOT real. The Israelites had now been slaves of the Canaanites for twenty long years and they knew only their one true God could save them (again). But how?

Deborah, an Israelite woman, was a judge. She was a very wise leader. She was also a friend of God, and she spoke with

Him often. He told her exactly what to do. The Israelites would come to her home in the mountains of Canaan for advice, and she taught them how to live right by loving each other and loving God with their whole hearts.

Deborah would sit in her mountain home crying out to God for help. She knew the Canaanites and their evil leader, Sisera, wanted to keep the Israelites enslaved and keep the Promised Land for themselves. Sisera led a very strong army of men who rode iron chariots pulled by huge horses. He used his army to bully the Israelites every day, and it was working. The Israelites were scared!

But the Lord had spoken words of hope to Deborah. She went to Barak, the leader of Israel's army, with a message from God. "The Lord said it's time to stand up against Sisera and the Canaanites," she told him.

But Barak refused. He thought it was ridiculous. "We will lose!" he shouted.

However, Deborah believed God. She said again, "The God of Israel has told you to fight against Sisera. You are to gather your men and fight the Canaanites, and the Lord says He will save Israel."

Barak still did not want to do it. He knew his army was much smaller than Sisera's and they did not have any chariots and hardly any weapons. Barak was sure there was no way they would win the battle. In fact, he was so sure it wouldn't work that he said, "The only way I will go into battle is if you, Deborah, lead my army!"

This didn't frighten Deborah, who was very brave. She did not back down. She knew what God had said. "Then I will do it!"

she said. "This is the day the Lord will save the Israelites from the Canaanites. The Lord has gone before you to fight your battle. But because you didn't trust that God would save Israel, God will have a woman win the battle!" Barak was left speechless.

So, Deborah bravely walked onto the battlefield with all of the Israelite soldiers behind her. They gasped as they saw Sisera and his many chariots and horses, but still, they ran into battle believing God would save them. The battle began.

At first, the Israelites were losing. They were not prepared to fight such a huge army. But suddenly, God sent a huge storm to the land. It rained so much that the land turned into a thick bog of mud and all of Sisera's chariots became stuck. They couldn't move! Then, the earth began to shake, and Sisera and his mighty warriors panicked, dropped their weapons, and ran away. The Lord showed Himself to be the one true God—the One who is in control of everything, including the storms and weather!

As the rain continued to fall and the Canaanite soldiers scattered, Sisera jumped off his swamped chariot and ran to find the closest place to hide from the Israelites. A Kenite woman named Jael ran out to meet him. She and her family lived in tents near the battlefield.

What Sisera didn't know was that, even though Jael was a Kenite, she was also a relative of Moses' wife. She was on the Israelites' side!

Jael knew this was her chance to kill this evil man and defeat the Canaanites once and for all. She knew she would have to trick him to make him trust her. So she said, "Come quickly! You will be safe in my tent!" When he asked for a drink, she gave him not only milk to drink, but also some meat to eat.

"Stand at the door and make sure no one tries to find me," Sisera said to Jael. "If anyone comes, tell them I'm not here." She agreed, covered him with a blanket, and told him to rest.

Jael knew this was her only chance. Once Sisera was fast asleep, she mustered up her courage and tiptoed over to

the sleeping warrior and killed him. When she saw Barak, the commander of the Israelite army, approaching her tent in search of Sisera, she ran out to meet him to tell him the good news. "Come," she told him, "and I will show you the man you are looking for!"

Deborah had been right all along: The Israelites defeated the Canaanites, just as the Lord said they would, and the victory came through the hands of a woman! With Sisera gone, the Israelites were now free to live in peace and worship their God, all because of the bravery of these two women. And, thanks to SHEROES Deborah and Jael, Israel had peace for the next forty years.

Devotion

1. Barak thought for sure that the small Israelite army would lose the battle against Sisera and his HUGE army. Have you ever thought a situation was too hard for God to handle because of how big it seemed to you?

2. God told Deborah that the Israelites would win the battle against Sisera and his army, but Barak did not believe God because the Israelite army was weaker and smaller. Have you ever felt afraid or worried about something because you didn't feel "big enough" or "smart enough" to do it?

3. Do you have trouble seeing people or problems the way God does? If so, ask God to help you begin to see people the way He does, through eyes of faith and not fear.

KYAH

SHERo of Judges, Chapter 9

*"...God punished Abimelech for the evil he had done against his father...
and his 70 brothers..."*

Judges 9:56 (NLT)

I n the days of the judges (like Deborah), Israel did not have any Kings. The nation relied on judges appointed by God to hear Him and lead the people.

One of Israel's judges was named Gideon. He was a good man who loved the Lord and helped Israel follow God. Gideon had seventy-one sons—that's a lot of kids! One of his sons, Abimelech, grew up to be an evil man.

Abimelech thought he was better than his father and brothers, and wanted more than anything to be ruler of Israel. However, he knew he would have to compete with his brothers for the job. So, after Gideon died, Abimelech gathered some other evil men and formed a plan to kill all seventy of his brothers. With all his brothers dead, Abimelech was sure to rule the land.

Sadly, Abimelech's plan worked, and he became ruler of Israel. Year after year, the Israelites were bullied by their new leader and his army. He was a violent man who stole their hard-earned money and made the people feel like slaves in their own land.

Finally, after three years, the Israelites could no longer take Abimelech's greediness and violence. In the dark of night, they met secretly in the town of Thebez to plan how they would kick Abimelech and his army out of Israel. Once their plan was complete, they began preparing for battle.

But Abimelech heard about the Israelites' secret plan. He was furious that anyone would consider fighting against him. He shouted to his men, "Let's go to the town of Thebez and surround the city and attack it!" He and his ruthless warriors rode all night long, in the bitter cold, to crush the Israelites' rebellion. In the blink of an eye, Abimelech and his militia circled the town, forced open the gates, and overtook Thebez.

The men, women, and children of Thebez ran for their lives to the top of a huge tower inside the city. They hid, hoping and praying that the tower would protect them. All the people of Thebez were frightened and held each other close, in hopes of protecting their loved ones from the horrible Abimelech and his mighty army. Thankfully, among the crowd was one very brave girl! The Bible doesn't tell us her name, so we will call her Kyah.

Just as Abimelech and his men were about to smash open the door at the bottom of the tower, Kyah looked over and saw a gigantic rock placed in a window at the top of the tower. It was hanging just over the entrance where Abimelech was. Suddenly, she had a brilliant idea!

Kyah felt hope for the first time, as she realized she might be able to stop Abimelech and his men. Looking at the rock, she bravely left her family to run to the open window. With all her strength, she pushed the large rock out of the window, and it fell from the top of the tower and landed on the wicked Abimelech!

No one could believe their eyes. Abimelech was dead! Once his army realized what had happened, they panicked and ran as fast as they could in all directions, fearing that the Israelites would attack them now that their leader was dead. Abimelech's army fled as fast as they had come!

The people of Thebez shouted and jumped for joy as they realized that their lives had been saved! God used Kyah to save the people of Thebez when everyone else was overcome by fear and did nothing. This SHEro's courage and trust in the Lord rescued God's people from the hands of their enemies and saved the lives of all her friends, family, and community!

Devotion

1. People in Kyah's village ran and hid in fear, and did nothing to stop the army that was coming to destroy them. Have you ever seen something happen that was not right, and did nothing about it?

2. Why do you think you did nothing to change the situation? If you are ever scared and do not know what to do, ask God to help you. God is SO much BIGGER than anything you will ever face.

3. Can you think of some ways you can help others when they are going through something difficult? (Some examples could be: writing them a note of encouragement or telling them how much they mean to you, or telling an adult if they are being bullied or hurt by someone.)

Ruth and Naomi

SHEroes of the Book of Ruth

"…I also know about everything you have done for your mother-in-law since the death of your husband. I have heard how you left your father and mother and your own land to live here among complete strangers."

Ruth 2:11 (NLT)

aomi was hungry and thirsty. Her lips were so dry, they were cracked. At this time, Israel was in a very bad drought, which meant there hadn't been rain for years. The Israelites could no longer grow food or feed their animals. Naomi knew that, soon, she and her household would have nothing to eat. She had no other choice but to move her family to another land. Hopefully, it would be a land where they could survive.

They packed up their belongings and soon found the land of Moab. *This is a good place to call home*, she thought. There,

Naomi, her husband, and their two sons settled. Eventually, their sons married Moabite women.

Time passed and Naomi's husband and two sons died, and the three women grieved the loss of the men they loved. Naomi and her daughters-in-law were left alone to take care of their large property and earn enough money to buy food. Naomi knew she didn't have enough money to take care of her daughters-in-law. Sadly, she told them they had to return to their families.

As tears ran down her face, Naomi said, "I pray that God will reward you for being so kind to me and my sons. I pray you find new husbands and a new beginning." She kissed them, and the three women wept and hugged each other. One daughter-in-law returned to her family, but Ruth, her other daughter-in-law, refused to leave.

"Wherever you go, I will go," Ruth told her. "Your people will be my people, and your God will be my God."

From then on, these two women formed a deep friendship with each other, and they continued to live together in the land of Moab.

Soon, a man traveling through Moab told Naomi that rain had finally returned to Israel! Naomi was thrilled! She longed to return to her homeland. Once again, Naomi told Ruth to return to her own family, but Ruth refused to leave. Together, they moved to an Israelite town called Bethlehem.

Because Naomi loved Ruth, she came up with a plan to make sure she would be taken care of—and the plan began with collecting leftover barley from the fields. Naomi had a relative named Boaz who loved the Lord. He was very rich and owned many barley fields. In Israel, farmers would often allow orphans and widows to pick up the grain the field workers missed, as a source of food. Naomi told Ruth to gather the leftover grain from Boaz' fields and bring it home for them to eat.

Day after day, Ruth would go to the fields, where the sun would beat down on her back as she picked up the leftover grain. It was hard work, but Ruth was committed to making sure she and Naomi had enough to eat.

Boaz took notice of Ruth's hard work. He admired how dedicated she was to helping her mother-in-law. He was very kind to her, even though she was a stranger from another land.

One day, Ruth sat down to eat after many long hours of laboring in the barley fields. With kindness in his eyes, Boaz approached Ruth and said, "I pray that God will repay you for your hard work, and that you will find protection in His mighty arms."

Then, he told his workers to drop grain on purpose so that Ruth would have more to collect and bring home. That day, she collected thirty-five pounds of barley! When Ruth returned home with the abundant load, Naomi said "God has not forgotten about us!"

After seeing her in his fields daily, Boaz began to fall in love with Ruth. At this time, the cultural customs were different than they are today. Because Boaz was much older than Ruth, Ruth would need to be the one to propose if they were to get married!

Ruth felt honored that Boaz has been so kind to her. She and Naomi often spoke about his generosity to them. Naomi could see that Boaz loved Ruth and she knew that he would be a kind and loving husband. Because she wanted the very best for Ruth, Naomi encouraged her to propose to Boaz.

Now, what happens next may seem a little silly to us, but it was common in Israel at the time. Ruth asked Boaz to marry her by laying down next to his feet in the middle of the night!

One evening, after dinner, Boaz lay down to sleep with some of his friends and workers, making his bed on a large pile of barley. At Naomi's instruction, Ruth dressed in her best clothes. The Bible says she was as beautiful in appearance as she was in her heart! As Naomi told her to do, she crept into the room where Boaz and his friends were sleeping and quietly lay down at his feet. She was exhausted from her long day of working in the sun, and soon she fell asleep.

When Boaz woke up, he rubbed his eyes and couldn't believe what he saw. This beautiful woman—the woman he loved—was lying at his feet! Boaz knew by her actions that Ruth wanted to marry him, and he was so happy! He gently touched her shoulder and said, "You are a kind and good woman. You could have chosen a younger man, poor or rich, but you chose me and I am honored. We shall be married."

So, Boaz and Ruth were married and, after some time passed, God gave them a son. As Naomi held her grandson in her arms for the first time, she looked at Ruth and said, "Praise the Lord that He has not forgotten about us!" With huge smiles on their faces, Ruth and Naomi giggled and joyfully thanked the Lord for all that He had done for them.

These two SHEROES had all their needs met and more because of their faith in God!

Devotion

1. Ruth and Naomi felt alone when their husbands died, and they moved to a country Ruth had never been to before. Have you ever felt lonely like Ruth or Naomi?

2. The Bible says in Joshua 1:9, "… Do not be afraid; do not be discouraged, for the LORD your God will be with you wherever you go." (NLT) God promises to never leave us, no matter how hard our circumstances are. How does that make you feel?

3. Can you think of anyone you know who may feel lonely?

4. What are some ways you can show God's love to people who may feel alone?

HANNAH

SHERO of 1 Samuel, Chapters 1-2

"... If you will look upon my sorrow and answer my prayer and give me a son, then I will give him back to you. He will be yours his entire lifetime."

1 Samuel 1:11(NLT)

Hannah had everything she wanted in life—except a child. She lived with her husband, Elkanah, in Ephraim, in the land of Israel. Hannah and Elkanah loved each other very much and wanted nothing more than to have children of their own. But the years passed, and no babies came.

Day after day, she watched her friends and family with their children. She would press her hands against her stomach and long to feel a baby kick inside of her. But, month after month passed, and Hannah was still not pregnant. To make things worse, women in her town said mean things to Hannah because she couldn't have children. Some days, she would lay in bed and cry because her heart felt so broken.

But, though Hannah was incredibly sad, she didn't lose faith in God. She believed God was good and that He had a plan for her life. His plan just looked different from her own.

One day, Hannah went to the temple to tell God what was on her heart. Tears ran down her cheeks as she cried out to God, "If you will think of me and give me a son, then I promise to give him back to you as a sacrifice, so he can serve you all the days of his life." Hannah gave God her desire for a son because she knew she could trust Him with her heart. She wanted a family more than anything, but her love for God was greater than what she wanted for herself.

That day, when Hannah left the temple, she had an over-whelming peace. She felt confident that God was in control of the situation—and of her life. She placed her desire for a child in the hands of her Heavenly Father, who was loving and kind, and her heart was lighter because of it.

But, do you know what? After a short time, Hannah began to feel a baby kicking inside of her tummy! After nine long months, she gave birth to a son she and Elkanah named Samuel. Her heart was filled with joy and her home was filled with laughter as they praised God for what He had given them. God had answered her prayer and given her the deepest desire of her heart! She would not forget her promise to the Lord—to give Samuel back to Him when the time was right.

For three years, Hannah fed Samuel when he was hungry, held him when he cried, and watched him take his first steps and say his first words. He grew from a baby to a toddler, and watching him was Hannah's dream come true. However, as much as she knew she would miss him, the time came for Hannah to follow through with her promise and bring Samuel back to the temple, where he could grow up in the presence of God. She bundled him up, packed a small bag with his favorite things, and they began their long journey.

As Hannah approached the temple, she bent down and kissed Samuel on the forehead. "I love you, my sweet boy," she told him as she ruffled his dark brown hair. "I will visit you as often as I can." They hugged once more and she left him in the care of Eli, the temple priest, trusting that God would take care of her son.

As Hannah left the temple, although she was sad, she felt joy deep inside of her, because she trusted that God was in control. She declared, "God, you are good! There is no one like You!" After so many years, He had given Hannah the desires of her heart. She felt honored to give her blessing back to Him. But then . . . God did something she didn't expect!

Because Hannah trusted God, He multiplied her dreams. He didn't just give her one child; He filled her home with many more children—not two, not three, but five more children, three more boys and two girls.

Hannah had faced such cruelty from women in her town, but she had never doubted that God loved her and had good plans for her and her family. Because of Hannah's faith, Samuel grew up in the temple knowing the love of his mother and the love of the Lord. In fact, from the time he was a little boy, God talked to Samuel and told him to remind the Israelites how much he loved them. Thanks to the faith of his mother, an amazing SHERO, Samuel grew up to be a prophet who changed the world.

Devotion

1. Hannah asked God for a child for many years. She waited and God answered her prayer with not just one child, but six children! God is SO generous! Is there something you have prayed about and have been waiting for, for a long time?
2. Are you still praying about it or have you seen that prayer answered?
3. What can we learn from Hannah about trusting God with our prayers?

ABIGAIL

SHERo of 1 Samuel, Chapter 25

"... And when the Lord has done these great things for you, please remember me, your servant."

1 Samuel 25:31 (NLT)

There once was a man in the land of Israel who was so foolish that the word "fool" became his name! He may have had another name, but he had such a bad reputation that everyone just called him Nabal, which means "fool."

Nabal was a selfish, angry, and evil man. He didn't care about anyone and treated everybody horribly. He was, however, very rich—he had three thousand sheep, one thousand goats, and huge fields of grain that stretched for miles and miles.

Nabal had a beautiful wife named Abigail and she was the exact opposite of him—she was kind, gentle, and wise. You may be wondering why she married such a wicked man! Well, at this time in Israel, women didn't get to choose the men they married; their parents chose for them. So Abigail was forced to marry Nabal because he could provide a home and food for her, but she didn't love him.

Little did Nabal or Abigail know, there was a brave man named David hiding in their land. He and his army of six hundred men were hiding from the jealous King of Israel, Saul. Have you ever heard the story of David and Goliath? You may remember that David, when he was young, struck down a huge giant named Goliath with just a small stone because the giant was bullying God's people and calling God names.

Later, God spoke to David through the prophet Samuel (Hannah's son!) and said that *David* would be the next King of Israel. King Saul was terrified that David would take his kingdom away from him. He hated him and wanted anyone who followed him dead! So David and his men were hiding in Nabal's tall grain.

As it turned out, Nabal's land was a great place to hide, so David and his men lived there for quite some time. Day and night, David and his army protected Nabal's shepherds and all who worked in his fields. His soldiers were like a wall around Nabal's property, defending all who lived there from the many thieves and wild animals who roamed the land. You'd think Nabal would be grateful, right?

When the grain had grown big and tall, Nabal's many servants collected it for him. David sent ten of his men to ask Nabal if he would share some of his grain with them, since he had more than enough. After all, David and his men had protected Nabal's servants and property for quite some time—and they were hungry! Their mouths watered as they thought of all the soft and delicious bread they could make from a portion of the grain collected.

But Nabal only laughed in the faces of David's men and said, "Who are you? I don't know you, and why should I share my food with you?"

David's men returned to him, discouraged, and told him how terribly Nabal had treated them. David was furious! Nabal was mean, rude, and selfish. David was not going to let him get away with it! So he said to his army, "Everyone come with me! Let's go to Nabal's home and teach him a lesson!"

David was angry and, as you know, it is never good to make decisions when you're angry. David wanted to hurt Nabal and everyone who lived in his house. He formed a plan with his men to raid the property and get rid of the horrible Nabal.

As David's men were preparing to attack Nabal's home, a servant boy ran desperately to Abigail for help. He was out of breath, but managed to say, "David and his men asked Nabal to share his food but he was awful to them! They have been so kind to us and have protected us day and night. I know that David and his men will punish Nabal for how he treated them. Please talk to David and try to change his mind!"

Abigail quickly ran to her kitchen and began cooking enough food for David and his six hundred men. (That probably took a long time!) She made bread and sweet cakes, packaged raisins and meat, and also prepared drinks for everyone. Exhausted after a long day of baking, she climbed onto her donkey and rode as fast as she could to meet David before his army arrived at her home.

When Abigail saw David, she jumped off her donkey and bowed low before him, saying, "Let this guilt fall on me! I'm sorry my husband treated you so horribly. I know God has chosen you to be the King over Israel. Please don't do something evil because you are angry. God's the one who fights our battles!"

David was humbled by Abigail's words, and he knew she was right. So he said to her, "Go in peace. You and your household will be safe."

Abigail was relieved and replied, "When God does great things for you, please remember me!"

David smiled kindly at Abigail. She made quite an impression on him! David and his men jumped on their horses and quickly went to find a new place to hide from King Saul. Abigail had saved the day! And do you know what happened next? God fought David's battle for him, just as Abigail had said, because soon after, Nabal grew extremely sick and died! Poor Abigail was left with the burden of Nabal's huge property and she was worried for her future. But, when David heard that Nabal was dead, he remembered Abigail's kindness, gentleness, and wisdom. He and his men returned to Nabal's land and he asked Abigail to marry him! Because of her humility, Abigail became the wife of King David and a SHEro for all of Israel!

Devotion

1. David was going to make a really bad choice to hurt Nabal and his entire household because he was angry. Have you ever made a decision when you were angry (or seen someone else do something foolish when they were angry)?
2. Do you remember when Abigail said to David, "Please don't do something evil because you are angry. God's the one who fights our battles!" How did God fight David's battle for him?
3. Can you think of a situation in your life in which you need God to fight for you?

Esther

SHEro of the Book of Esther

"...Who knows if perhaps you were made Queen for just such a time as this?..."

Esther 4:14 (NLT)

Esther—a beautiful young Jewish woman—was an orphan. Her parents died when she was little, and Mordecai, her cousin, looked after her. He became like a father to her. Esther was known throughout the land for her beauty. In fact, she stood out from all the other women.

At this time, the Jews (whom many people called the Israelites) were prisoners in their own land. Again. They lived under the rule of the kingdom of Persia. Persia had a King, but every King needs a Queen. One day, the King summoned his servants to his palace. "Go into every village, town, and city to find me the most beautiful women in all of Persia," he told them.

The servants obeyed and began the search for a Queen. They went into every town and village in Israel, searching for the most beautiful women they could find. They had been told to take the women from their families, whether the women wanted to go or not, and bring them to the palace so they could learn the ways of royalty. They would be given fancy clothes to wear and be bathed in fancy perfumes. After one year in the palace, the King would choose only one woman to become his wife.

Esther was chosen by the King's servants to be one of the many women brought to live in the palace for an entire year. As Esther was forced from Mordecai's arms, he kissed her cheek and whispered in her ear, "Do not tell anyone you are a Jew. You could be treated very badly if you do." Esther was frightened, but she obeyed her cousin and bravely left her family behind to live in the palace of the King.

After one year, the chosen women were presented to the King of Persia. One by one, they were brought to him for his approval. As soon as the King saw Esther, he thought she was the most beautiful woman he had ever seen. Immediately, he knew he wanted Esther to be the Queen of Persia. All the while, Esther hid her true identity from the King and his servants. No one in the palace knew she was a Jew.

Soon, Esther was made Queen of Persia. One day, one of the King's most respected men, Haman, rode through the streets near the palace, as he did almost every day. As always, everyone bowed low to honor him. But on this day, one man refused to bow. Mordecai. He knew the truth about Haman—that he was an evil man who hated the Jews and wanted them gone from Persia for good! So, Mordecai stood tall with his head held high and refused to bow.

"How dare you!" Haman shouted with anger. He was furious that someone would refuse to bow, especially a Jew! He went to the King and said, "These foolish Jews do not respect the laws of Persia. They think they're better than us. We should get rid of them!"

The King agreed to the plan, and Haman made an order: In a year's time, Persian soldiers will kill every Jew and take everything they own. Little did Haman know, Mordecai had sent a message to warn Esther. The message said, "My dear Esther, you must do something! Your people are in danger. The Lord made you the Queen of Persia so you can save our people!"

Esther was terrified. She knew she could be killed because she was a Jew, too! She also knew that anyone who went to speak to the King without his permission could be killed—even his own Queen.

But soon, God's peace came over Esther and she knew what she had to do—trust His plan for her and her people. She took a deep breath and wrote to Mordecai. "I will do it. If I die, I die. But please have our people pray for me, because I am scared."

Esther prayed for favor in the eyes of the King. She felt strengthened knowing her people were praying for her, too. When she had gathered her courage, she pushed open the magnificent doors at the palace and stepped into the King's throne room. Shaking, she knew the King could order her to be killed at any moment. She let out a deep sigh of relief when her royal husband held out his golden scepter, giving her permission to approach him. She had found favor in the King's eyes, just as she and her people had prayed for! The King said to her, "What can I give you? I will give you anything you wish, even half of my kingdom!"

Esther held back tears and told him the real reason she had come to see him. She confessed that she was a Jew, and begged him not to let Haman destroy her people.

The King was surprised to find out that his wife was a Jew, but he did not reject her. He fumed with anger toward Haman, not toward Esther! He decided to trick Haman by throwing him a huge banquet in his honor so Haman could be arrested at the party. When Haman walked into the banquet, his head was held high with arrogance and pride. He loved that the King had thrown him such a beautiful party. But Haman was shocked when the King announced that Esther was a Jew and that Haman would be arrested for trying to kill the Queen. The King's soldiers marched Haman out of the room to his death.

God had indeed made Esther the Queen of Persia so His people could be rescued! Even today, every year, Jewish people everywhere celebrate the Feast of Purim to remember Esther's bravery and God's love for His people. They celebrate this feast for two days, eating delicious food and giving each other gifts. Their hearts are continually filled with thanksgiving because their people were saved from death.

Because of Esther's bravery and faith in God, this SHEro helped save God's people. God rescued the Jews and entire generations of people because of her obedience and sacrifice.

Devotion

1. Mordecai told Esther that God had made her to be Queen to save the lives of all the Jews. Do you know that God made you for a purpose, too? He did! There is a reason you are alive, and God wants to move through you to change the world for the better! Is it difficult for you to believe that God has a great plan for your life?

2. Esther was afraid to go into the King's throne room, but she knew God was asking her to do the right thing and trust Him. Have you ever felt scared to do the right thing?

3. Esther, Mordecai, and all the Israelites celebrated because their lives had been saved. What are some ways you can celebrate what God has done in your life?

4. Thanking God for all He has done for you is one way you can celebrate! What are some things in your life that you want to thank God for?

SHEROES
of the *Bible*

WOMEN OF THE NEW TESTAMENT

Elizabeth

SHEro of the Gospel of Luke, Chapter 1

"When Elizabeth heard Mary's greeting, the baby leaped in her womb, and Elizabeth was filled with the Holy Spirit."

Luke 1:41 (NIV)

For four hundred years, God was silent—that is a really long time! There were no prophets. No new scriptures written. No new "words from the Lord."

During this time of silence, a Jewish woman named Elizabeth lived with her husband Zechariah in the charming hill country of Judea. On this particular day, she sat at her window, looking out over the rolling green hills and colorful flowers that danced in the breeze. Elizabeth had experienced much joy in her life, but sadness cast a shadow because, unlike most women in her village, she could not have children. Now she was getting older, and it was almost too late to think about it anymore.

Elizabeth sighed. She didn't want God to think she was complaining. She was thankful for her kind and loving husband, who was a priest in the temple in Jerusalem. He had helped her hold her head high when people in their village whispered about her because she did not have children. As she looked out the window, Elizabeth thanked the Lord for all the ways He had blessed her life. No matter what anyone else said, she knew she was loved and treasured by God.

Elizabeth jumped as the bedroom door slammed behind her! It was Zechariah, and he was in a hurry to get to the temple. This was an exciting day, because he had been chosen to participate in a special ceremony that happened only once a year. Most priests only had this opportunity once in their lifetime—and today was his day! Elizabeth was thrilled to accompany her husband, and she looked forward to witnessing this important occasion from the crowd that gathered outside the temple gates.

It was difficult to see everything from where Elizabeth stood, but it was clear that not one person thought that God would actually show up. Remember, God had been silent for four hundred years. The people came year after year to the temple, but no one ever thought that God would speak.

Zechariah spoke to the crowd, then turned and entered the temple. He was in there a long time, so people began to whisper to each other, wondering if something bad might have happened to him while he was inside. Elizabeth began to worry, too, when suddenly her husband emerged. He looked like he had seen a ghost! He gestured with his hands, pointing to the entrance of the temple. When he opened his mouth to talk, nothing came out. It was clear to everyone that he had seen something so spectacular, so amazing, that he could no longer speak! Everyone wondered, *Had God spoken to him while he was inside the temple?*

On their journey home, Zechariah shared with Elizabeth what had happened. He still had no voice, so he had to write it down for her to read. Elizabeth could not believe what the paper said! Zechariah wrote that an angel named Gabriel had appeared to him! The angel told him, "Don't be afraid, Zechariah! God has heard your prayer. Your wife will give you a son, and you are to name him John. You and many others will rejoice at his birth, for he will be great in the eyes of God. He will be filled with the Holy Spirit even before his birth and will prepare God's people for the coming of the Lord."

Zechariah said to the angel, "How can I be sure this will happen? My wife and I are old!"

The angel said, "I am Gabriel, and I stand in the very presence of God. But, since you did not believe me, you will be unable to speak until the child is born."

Elizabeth could not believe her eyes! Was it true? Was she going to be a mother at last? She burst into happy tears, shouting, "God has taken away my embarrassment and is giving me a child!" Elizabeth put her hands on her stomach and thanked God for how good he was to her.

For many months, people gossiped about Zechariah and Elizabeth. They whispered that Zechariah was silent because he was under a curse. They questioned if he had really heard from God. But Elizabeth firmly supported her husband. Her faith never failed. Month after month, she watched her belly grow bigger and bigger, and every month she celebrated and thanked God.

One day, as Elizabeth was in her kitchen preparing dinner, she heard a knock on her door. To her surprise, it was her cousin, Mary—from Nazareth—who was also pregnant. As soon as she saw Mary, Elizabeth's baby jumped for joy inside her belly. Mary's baby was Jesus, the promised Rescuer from God. It was like Elizabeth's baby recognized God's Son! Suddenly, Elizabeth was filled with the Holy Spirit and said to Mary, "God has blessed you above all women! Why am I so honored that the mother of my Lord should visit me? You are blessed because you believed that the Lord would do what He said!"

Mary stayed with Elizabeth and Zechariah for three months and then returned to her home. Soon afterward, Elizabeth's baby was born, and the entire village came to celebrate his birth. When asked what they were to name him, Zechariah wrote the name "John," as the angel had directed.

"John?" questioned all the people. "No one in your family is named John. Why would you give him that name?"

Elizabeth stepped up to defend her husband and the name the Lord had given him for the baby. "His name is John," she agreed. Elizabeth held John and looked at his precious face with pride as she pondered what God would do with her baby's life.

Immediately after the baby was named, Zechariah could speak again. He, too, was filled with the Holy Spirit and began praising God for the gift that John was to the world. He said, "You, my little son, will be called the prophet of the most high God, because you will prepare the way for the Lord!"

Throughout the Judean hills, all who heard of John's birth wondered, "What will this child turn out to be? The hand of the Lord is obviously on him in a special way!"

*****

After John's cousin, Jesus was born, the King of Israel made a terrible decree. He ordered all the baby boys under two years old to be killed. He had seen the star announcing the birth of God's Promised Rescuer—a new "King"—and he was afraid for his throne.

When they heard of the King's order, Elizabeth and Zechariah fled with their son to the desert, to hide him from the King's soldiers. There, John grew up in the wilderness and became strong in spirit. It was in the desert that Elizabeth taught John the Scriptures. When John was an adult, God called him out of the desert to declare to Israel that their Promised Rescuer, Jesus, was coming soon!

Elizabeth, through her faithfulness to her God, her husband, her cousin, and her son, was a SHERo whom God used to prepare the way for Jesus!

Devotion

1. Elizabeth offered her home as a safe place for Mary when she was pregnant and scared. She also supported her husband when other people questioned him and gossiped about him. How can you be a safe place for someone who is going through a hard time? Or a safe place for someone whom others are criticizing?

2. When Elizabeth saw Mary, she celebrated what God was doing in Mary's life. Is there a friend or family member with whom you can celebrate about something good happening in their lives? How can you help them celebrate?

3. Elizabeth taught John the Scriptures, which helped him grow strong in his relationship with God. How can reading the Scriptures—the Bible—help you grow stronger in your own relationship with God?

MARY, THE MOTHER OF JESUS

SHERo of the Gospels

"I am the Lord's servant. May everything you have said about me come true."

Luke 1:38 (NLT)

It was a regular day, like any other day, in the small town of Nazareth in Galilee. In a simple home that had been carved out of the hillside, a teenaged girl named Mary was on her knees, scrubbing the stone floor and humming quietly to herself.

As she scrubbed, she could not help but think about how her life would soon change, and she was nervous! She was engaged to marry an older man named Joseph. Her family, being poor, hoped to marry her to a man who could provide for her, and Joseph was the answer to their prayers. But Mary wasn't so sure.

Joseph was a kind and honorable man, but was she really ready to get married?

Suddenly a bright light filled the room and a huge figure appeared. It was the angel, Gabriel! Mary was so shocked and frightened that she fell backward, knocking over her bucket of dirty water. The angel said, "Don't be afraid, Mary. God wants to bless you! You will become pregnant with a son, and you will name him Jesus. He will be called the Son of God. He is the deliverer the world has been waiting for."

Mary was so stunned she could not speak! *How can this be happening to me?* she thought, her heart beating wildly.

Finally, she managed to respond. "But I'm not even married yet! How can this be?"

Gabriel smiled and said kindly but firmly, "The Holy Spirit will come upon you in power, and you will become pregnant. Nothing is impossible with God!"

A strange sense of peace came over Mary. She trusted what the angel was saying. Though she was still a bit scared she said, "I am God's servant. I will do whatever He asks me to do." She felt honored that God would choose her out of all of the women in the world to be the mother of God's Son.

Sure enough, everything happened just as the angel said it would. Soon, Mary was pregnant. At this time in Israel, if people found out that Mary was pregnant but not married yet, they would punish her, and maybe even sentence her to death!

So, Mary ran for her life to the hill country of Judea to be with her cousin, Elizabeth, who was also expecting a baby. There, Mary stayed for three months until Elizabeth's son, John, was born. Those three months were a blessing to Mary as she found safety in her cousin's cozy cottage.

She knew she needed to return to her village, but Mary feared what Joseph and the people in her village would think, and rightly so. After she returned, her pregnant belly grew and people began to snicker and gossip. She was so embarrassed!

When Mary told Joseph that she was pregnant, at first he didn't want to marry her anymore. However, that night, God gave Joseph a dream. In the dream, God said, "Joseph, do not be afraid to take Mary home as your wife. The baby inside of her is from the Holy Spirit. She will give birth to a son, and you will give Him the name Jesus, because He will save His people." When Joseph woke up, he did what God asked him to do, and he married Mary.

Some time passed, and God chose what seemed to be an awkward time for Jesus to be born. Mary and Joseph were on a road trip! The government forced them—and many other people—to travel ninety miles, a three to four-day journey, to the town of Bethlehem to check in with their governor. Mary was riding on the back of a dirty old donkey when her labor pains started.

It was a busy time in Bethlehem, and the streets were bustling with people because of the government's order. Because of this, there were no rooms available anywhere. Mary moaned in pain, and Joseph begged for help from everyone they passed. He was scared— he had never delivered a baby before!

Why did God have me do this now? Mary thought to herself. Her labor pains were increasing. It was time.

Eventually, they met a man who allowed them to stay in his barn. The barn was cold, dirty, and filled with all kinds of animals. Mary settled down and made a bed out of straw. There, she delivered her brand-new baby son, and the Holy Spirit filled them both.

As Mary cradled Jesus in her arms, she looked into His eyes. She could see how much He loved her, and it took her by surprise. She knew Jesus was special and that He had come to save her and her people. She did not know what His life would look like, but she knew the presence of God was in Him and He would change people's lives forever.

As Jesus grew, Mary watched Him perform countless miracles. She saw Him multiply bread and fish so that thousands of hungry people could eat. She watched in amazement as He healed people from every kind of sickness and disease. He even raised people from the dead! It took only the touch of His tender hand, and they were healed. She was in awe of her son and loved Him with her whole heart.

News about Jesus spread far beyond the borders of Galilee, and soon the sick were traveling from miles away just to be touched by Jesus. Large crowds followed Him wherever He went. Soon, the crowds became so large that Mary was unable to see her son up close. The crowds slowly pushed her out of the way.

God gently reminded Mary that she would need to let Jesus go so He could do all that God had asked Him to do. Jesus was not just her son; He was God's son. Mary realized that though Jesus was the sweetest gift, He was not just her gift, but a gift for the whole world. For this SHEro, trusting God with her son was the hardest thing she had ever done.

The day arrived when Jesus was arrested by people who hated Him. Mary watched from the crowd and cried as she saw her son suffer. *How could this be God's plan?* she thought. But God did indeed have a plan, a plan that was better than Mary could have ever imagined.

Three days after Jesus died, Mary and a few women went to the tomb where Jesus' body had been placed after His death. But when they arrived, they found it empty, with two angels outside of it! One of the angels said, "Don't be so surprised! Jesus is no longer here. He has been raised from the dead!"

As they ran toward town, Jesus appeared to them Himself. He playfully said, "Hi, ladies!" Mary immediately dropped her things and ran to Him! She hugged Him and kissed His face, crying happily because God had kept His promise.

Mary eventually had to say good-bye to Jesus again, when He returned to Heaven, but this time it was different. He assured her that He would send His Holy Spirit to be with her always. Mary would never be alone again!

Jesus makes the same promise to us. Jesus is alive and His Holy Spirit is with us always! He wants to use people like you and me to help care for and heal our broken world. Because of the Holy Spirit in us, we can be SHEROES, too, just like Mary!

Devotion

1. Mary loved Jesus so much that she wanted Him all to herself. God gently reminded Mary that He came not just for her, but for the whole world. There is enough of God for everyone to enjoy! What are some ways that you enjoy spending time with Jesus?

2. God gave Mary the gift of being Jesus' mother. God can do Big Things through you too! If you could choose, how would you want God to use you to change the world?

3. After Jesus died and rose again, He sent His Holy Spirit into the hearts of EVERYONE who calls on the name of Jesus. Do you want Him to live inside of your heart, too? All you have to do is believe in Jesus—that He is God's Promised Rescuer, to save the world (and all of us) from sin and death. If you are willing to say that you believe in Him, Jesus will send His Holy Spirit to live in your heart. If you ask Him, you will have a Best Friend inside you who will never leave you, ever!

Anna

SHEro of the Gospel of Luke, Chapter 2

"... She never left the Temple but stayed there day and night, worshiping God with fasting and prayer."

Luke 2:37 (NLT)

The morning light beamed through a crack in a shuttered window onto Anna's sleeping face. Gently, a soft breeze blew across her wrinkled cheeks, waking her. She heard a familiar voice whisper, "Anna . . . I have a gift for you today." This was not a voice she heard with her ears. This was a voice she heard in her *spirit.*

Anna's eyes opened slowly. She rubbed them and yawned. She knew that voice! It was God's! He often woke her up early with a gentle whisper, calling her to come spend time with Him. Anna loved serving God at the temple—for most of her long life, she had spent much of her time there.

But this morning, God had a surprise for her. *What could the gift be?* Anna wondered to herself. She was so excited! She believed something special would happen today—she just didn't know what! Quickly, she got dressed and rushed to the temple. She didn't even eat breakfast. Anna often skipped meals so she could pray and spend more time with God.

Anna's favorite thing in the entire world was to be in God's presence. Being with Him brought her the deepest joy her heart had ever known. She had married young, like most women in Israel in her time. But, sadly, her husband had died suddenly, after only seven years of marriage. Anna's heart was broken, and she turned to God for comfort and healing. He found her in her sadness.

God was loving and kind to Anna. Year after year, He made sure she had everything she needed, just like a good father does for his children. Even the temple priests took pity on her, and gave her a place to stay and food to eat.

Through her many years spent with God, Anna learned how to hear His voice, and He taught her how to pray for God's people. While praying, she often felt like a watchman on the city walls, protecting people from danger. Her job was important. She would boldly pray promises from the Old Testament, declaring God's love and protection over His people. She felt empowered and strong, and she knew she was doing God's work!

Many of the Old Testament promises Anna prayed were about the coming Savior of Israel. For hundreds of years, the people had been waiting for their Promised Rescuer, who would deliver them from all of their enemies. They did not know who it would be or when He would come, but they waited expectantly.

On this day, as Anna arrived eagerly at the temple, she heard voices. She peeked into a room nearby and saw a man and a young girl holding a newborn baby. They were dedicating him to God! As soon as she saw the baby, Anna heard God's voice whisper in her spirit, "This baby is the gift you've been waiting for, Anna." In that instant, she knew this baby was the long-awaited Savior of Israel.

Boldly, she approached the young mother. "Hello," Anna said kindly. "I'm Anna. Your baby is beautiful. May I hold Him and speak a blessing over Him?"

"Yes," replied the girl. She felt she could trust this gentle old woman. As she handed over the baby for a blessing, the girl said, "My name is Mary, and this is my husband, Joseph." She smiled lovingly at her baby, who was fast asleep. "And this is Jesus."

Gently, Anna lifted the baby boy from Mary's arms and thanked God for this gift from Heaven. She just stared at him— He was beautiful in every way. Anna knew in her heart that He was going to change the world, just like she had prayed.

This SHEro could not contain her excitement! God chose Anna to be the first woman to tell her people that the Savior had arrived. The Rescuer of Israel had been born in Bethlehem, just as the Old Testament prophets had said. Anna felt honored that God had chosen her to see the Savior with her own eyes. She couldn't wait to share the good news!

Devotion

1. Anna had a close relationship with God because she talked to Him all the time. She told Him about the good and the bad things happening in her life. What are some things you would like to talk to God about?
2. Prayer is simply talking to God. Take a few minutes to tell God what is going on in your life.
3. Anna waited for a long time for the gift of Jesus. Is there something you've been waiting for God to do? Ask God to give you the patience and faith to believe that He will do it.

PHOTINI (WOMAN AT THE WELL)

SHERO of John, Chapter 4

"Then, leaving her water jar, the woman went back to the town and said to the people, 'Come, see a man who told me everything I ever did...'"

John 4: 28-29 (NIV)

I t was one of the hottest days of the year. Photini's[1] hair was sticking to her back and her clothes were soaked with sweat. She had traveled a great distance to get water from a well outside of town. She walked a long way in the scorching heat

---

1   John, who wrote this story in his Gospel, does not tell us the name of the woman of Samaria whom Jesus met at the well. But later church historians suggest that, after she became a follower of Jesus, the disciples named her "Photini," which means "enlightened one."

to lower her bucket into a hole and collect the water from deep inside the ground. It was not an easy job.

It was noon and the desert sun in Samaria beamed fiercely. Exhausted from her journey, Photini sat on a large rock next to the well. It seemed like a good place to rest.

Suddenly, she was interrupted by a lovely sound. Photini looked up and saw a bird singing as it flew through the clear blue sky. As she watched, Photini wished that she were as happy as that little bird. She wished that she had something joyful to sing about.

But life for Photini was not so joyful. She looked to her right and to her left, and as usual, there was no one to be seen. It was always so quiet at the well—too quiet. This silence was something Photini was used to. She was always alone.

The women from her village usually traveled together to collect water from the well. Early every morning, Photini heard them chatting as they passed by her window. But she was never invited to join. In fact, most mornings Photini could hear them talking badly about her.

In their culture, women were married once—maybe twice, if their first husband had died. But Photini had been married five different times and was now with another man. The women made fun of Photini and shamed her for having had so many husbands. She did everything alone, from shopping at the village market to collecting water from the well.

Alone again in the quiet and the heat, she sat listening to the sweet bird's song.

But wait! In the distance she saw a man chatting with friends as they traveled toward town. Photini did not know it yet, but she was about to meet Jesus!

The dry, hot breeze caused the dust to stir around His feet as He walked. Jesus and His friends were caught up in a great conversation when, in the distance, Jesus noticed Photini. Immediately, the Holy Spirit spoke to His heart, and He knew that Photini was the reason He had traveled to that town.

His heart was filled with compassion for her. Even from where He was, He could sense her sadness.

Jesus told His friends to continue without Him. He walked toward the well, near where Photini was sitting. Tired and thirsty from His journey, He sat down on a patch of dry grass and asked her, "May I have something to drink?"

In that culture, a man did not talk to a woman who was not his wife. Yet, Jesus spoke to Photini. On top of that, she was a Samaritan, and He was a Jew, and their tribes did not get along with each other. They should have been enemies!

But here was Jesus, purposely asking a Samaritan woman for water. Photini was surprised and took a moment to respond.

"But you are a Jew," she said with a shaky voice, "and I am a Samaritan woman. How can you ask me for a drink?" Jesus looked at her tenderly and said, "If you ask me, I will give you *living water*."

Photini was confused. Jesus had no bucket. What did He mean?

Jesus gestured to the well and answered, "Everyone who drinks from this well will still be thirsty, but whoever drinks the water I give them will never be thirsty again." Jesus was saying that just as our bodies need water to live, our hearts need His Holy Spirit. He is the only one who can fill our hearts and satisfy our needs.

Photini looked into Jesus' eyes. She still did not understand, but she was moved by His kindness to her. Jesus knew that Photini needed God to heal her sadness. "I know you are so lonely, and that you have had five husbands and are now living with another man."

Photini's eyes widened. She was speechless. This man was a stranger, yet somehow, He knew all about her life! She began to feel God's love fill her body.

Suddenly, she remembered something she had learned as a child—that God had promised He would send a Rescuer to save the world. Had God been talking about this man? Filled with excitement, Photini said, "I know that our Rescuer is coming soon, and I can't wait to meet Him!"

Jesus smiled. "You just did. I am the One you have been waiting for!"

Photini dropped her bucket and ran all the way back to her village as quickly as her legs could carry her. This SHERO could not wait to tell everyone that the One they had been waiting for was finally here!

For the first time in a long time, people actually listened to Photini. They even followed her back to the well, where Jesus was still waiting.

The well was not so quiet anymore. The air buzzed as everyone talked to Jesus and asked Him questions. Photini looked around the crowd and realized that she was no longer alone. Her heart was full, and she smiled because she knew her life would never be the same.

Photini became a SHERO to her entire village because she chose to share Jesus with them. In her loneliness, she could have kept Him all to herself. Instead, she wanted everyone to meet the One who had healed her heart. Because of Photini, others got to know the "living water" of the Holy Spirit, and their hearts would never thirst again!

Devotion

1. Photini did not have any friends. Do you ever wish that you had more friends?
2. Jesus wants you to know that you are never alone because He will always be your friend.
3. Is there someone in your neighborhood or at school who does not have many friends? How can you be a friend to them? Have you ever thought that maybe you are an answer to their prayer?

MARTHA AND MARY

SHEROES of the Gospels

"A dinner was prepared in Jesus' honor. Martha served, and Lazarus was among those who ate with him. Then Mary took a twelve-ounce jar of expensive perfume made from essence of nard, and she anointed Jesus' feet with it, wiping his feet with her hair. The house was filled with the fragrance."

John 12:2-3 (NLT)

The smell of freshly baked bread and sweet fig jam filled the air of Martha and Mary's home. They lived in Bethany, near Jerusalem, where olive groves and fig trees lined the horizon of every hillside. As children, Mary, Martha, and their brother Lazarus often played at the Mount of Olives. They broke branches off the olive trees and chased each other through the thickets.

They had such wonderful memories as children, but now they were grown and their parents were gone. Martha was in charge of their home and property. She often felt worried about money and overwhelmed by all she had to do to make sure her family was provided for. Mary and Lazarus were helpful with chores, but sometimes it didn't feel like enough.

Martha loved to host parties at their home. She would cook lots of food, and she, her siblings, and their guests would talk long into the night. Parties made her feel like a child again. It was a big job to cook for these events, and she often found herself in her kitchen for hours, rushing around to make everything perfect.

Today, they were expecting a special guest. Jesus! Martha and Mary and Lazarus had become His close friends, and He was always an honored guest in their home. He frequently stayed with them when He was in Jerusalem. Knowing He was coming, Martha had spent the day baking bread, cooking fig jam, and pressing olives into oil.

When Jesus arrived, He greeted everyone with a gentle smile. He was the kindest person Martha knew. Mary and Lazarus were right by her side to greet Him, and they quickly motioned for Him and His friends to get comfortable in their dining room. They listened as He shared story after story of how God's love had healed the most broken bodies and hearts. They sat at His feet and listened.

As Mary and Lazarus sat listening to Jesus with the others, Martha was busy in the kitchen. As much as Martha loved hosting the party, she began to get frustrated with her sister and wanted her to help. Martha was so annoyed that she said to Jesus, "Please tell Mary to get up and come help me in here!"

Jesus looked at Martha and said, "Martha, you are worried about so many things. Mary is choosing to spend time with me instead of in the kitchen, and that's a good thing."

Jesus was right. Martha was worried about a lot of things, but the one thing that would bring her peace was to spend time with Him. Jesus came many more times to visit Martha, Mary and Lazarus. They were the best of friends.

One day, Lazarus got very sick. He could not eat or get out of bed for days. Martha sent a letter to Jesus asking Him to come help, but when He arrived four days later, it was too late. Lazarus had died.

While Jesus was on the road to their home, Martha ran to meet Him and fell at His feet saying, "If only you had been here, my brother would not have died! But I know God will do whatever you ask…"

Jesus looked lovingly at her and said, "Oh, Martha, those who believe in Me will live, even if they die. Do you believe this?"

This was her moment of decision. Did she really trust Jesus? Did she really believe He was who He said He was?

This SHERO looked up at Him and answered, "Yes! I believe you are the Christ, the Son of God."

Mary came running, too. She hugged Jesus tightly, then fell to His feet on the bumpy road and cried, "If you had been here my brother would not be dead!" When Jesus saw her weeping, He was deeply moved. Lazarus was His friend and He loved him. Jesus began to cry, too.

The sisters led Jesus to where Lazarus had been buried. A large stone covered the cave, and Jesus asked for the stone to be moved. Jesus said, "Didn't I say that if you believed, you would see the glory of God?" Then He looked up, and said softly, "Thank You, God, for what You are about to do!"

Looking into the cave, Jesus called, "Lazarus, come out!"

In an instant, Lazarus came out of the cave with his hands and feet still wrapped in cloth. He looked a little confused. Everyone was shocked. Mary and Martha cried with joy as they ran to their brother with open arms. He was alive!

Everyone there, even those who had not believed in Jesus before, believed in Him now. He not only healed people who were sick, but He brought the dead back to life!

It was time to celebrate. Martha cooked yummy food and invited everyone to another party. Jesus and His friends ate together, with Lazarus close by His side. They thanked God for His kindness and power.

While they were eating dinner, Mary quietly got up and went to a room where she kept a jar of expensive perfume. This jar belonged to their family and was worth a lot of money—as much money as they made in a whole year! This SHERO was so filled with love for Jesus that she took the bottle, kneeled down in front of everyone, and poured the perfume onto His feet. And just like that, the Holy Spirit filled the room.

There were some there who felt Mary was wasting her money by pouring all of the perfume on Jesus, but Martha knew that Jesus was worth it. Martha, who used to be so worried about money, loved that Mary gave it all so freely to Jesus.

He was special. Martha and Mary had no regrets. They did not mind giving everything they had to show Jesus how much they loved Him.

After Jesus died, these two SHEROES told everyone about His love and the things He had taught them. And they are counted for all of history as two of His dearest friends!

Devotion

1. Martha worried about many things, like taking care of her family. Are there things that you worry about? Take a moment to give those things to Jesus and ask Him to help bring you the same peace that He gave Martha.

2. Mary and Martha showed their love for Jesus in different ways. Mary loved to spend time with Jesus and Martha loved to do things for Him. Jesus loved how both Mary and Marth showed their love for Him. Is it easier for you to spend time with Jesus or to do things for Him and others?

3. One way may come more naturally to you, but God loves us to do both. What are some ways you can spend time with Jesus like Mary? What are some ways you can do things for Jesus and others, like Martha?

Mary Magdalene

SHEro of the Gospels

"Mary Magdalene found the disciples and told them, 'I have seen the Lord!...'"

John 20:18 (NLT)

One day, Jesus walked into the busy fishing town of Magdala, where the air was salty and smelled like smoked fish. Magdala was known for its beautifully dyed wool and people would travel from all over the region to buy items that were made there. This thriving city was filled with markets that sold very interesting and unique items.

While the streets of Magdala were buzzing with business, one mother sat inside her home worrying about her daughter, Mary. (Because she was from the city of Magdala, history remembers her as "Mary Magdalene.")

Mary's mind was sick. She felt all kinds of feelings—she would be angry, then suddenly sad, or laughing and then afraid. No one could understand her because nothing she said made any sense. Mary had nightmares every night and daytime was no better. Her family had asked for help from many doctors, but no one could help her. Even though Mary's family loved her very much, she always felt alone and misunderstood.

As Jesus walked the streets of Magdala, He heard God tell Him to go to Mary's house. He came to her door, with a large crowd trailing behind him. He lovingly placed His finger on His lips to quiet the crowd, and He knocked on the front door. Almost immediately, a very tired woman, with graying hair and worry lines around her eyes, appeared in the doorway—Mary's mother.

When her sad eyes looked at Jesus, hope leaped inside her. She knew who this was! This was the man who had healed so many people! She knew immediately why He had come. She led Jesus by the hand to her daughter's room.

Mary lay in bed with her eyes closed and her body tense as her mind frantically searched for peace. Her messy hair and crinkled forehead showed that she was exhausted and confused.

But when Jesus looked at Mary, He saw her as God created her to be—a joyful woman who would bring hope to many people. He wanted her to know freedom and a full life.

Jesus lovingly said, "Mary." When He said her name, the Holy Spirit flooded the room like a tidal wave. It pushed out all the fear, anger, and sadness that had been there for so long. His voice was beautiful and kind. In an instant, her mind and body felt calm.

As Mary opened her eyes, she saw Jesus kneeling beside her bed with a smile that would brighten the darkest night. Mary could not help but smile back because her heart was full for the first time.

Mary got up out of her bed and fell to her knees beside Jesus. He had healed her mind when no one else could! She said, "I am yours forever!" She promised to follow Him and leave everything else behind, even her home and family.

From that day forward, Mary gave all her time and money to provide food and shelter for Jesus and His followers. She became a SHEro to all who knew her. She gave everything she owned to help those who were hurting. Her town, nation, and even the surrounding countries were changed because of her generosity. She loved others because she had been loved first by the God of the universe.

As Mary spent more and more time with Jesus, she watched in amazement as His touch healed the sickest of bodies. But there were those who did not like Jesus' miracles. They chose to crucify Him on a cross.

You might think this is the end . . . but God had a different plan.

A few days later after Jesus died, as the sun rose over the city of Jerusalem, Mary approached the cave where Jesus was buried. She saw that the large stone, which had been placed in front of the entrance, had been moved and now the cave was open. She rushed into the cave and saw that Jesus' body was gone! She was scared because she thought someone had stolen His body.

As she started to panic, she looked up and saw two angels. "Why are you afraid?" they asked her.

Her voice trembled and she said, "I don't know where they have put Jesus' body!" Suddenly, out of the corner of her eye, she saw a man standing outside of the cave. She ran to him, thinking he might know where Jesus was taken.

The kind man saw the tears running down her face and softly asked, "Why are you crying?" As she buried her face in her hands, she heard the man say her name, "Mary."

With that one word, joy took over her heart. She knew that voice! This was the same voice that had said her name long ago when all the darkness left her. "Jesus!" she shouted. She threw her arms around Him and hugged Him tightly. The Savior she loved and thought was dead was alive!

They laughed and cried together as they recalled everything that happened over the last few days. Mary could not take her eyes off of Jesus. He looked different somehow, even more radiant than before. "Go and tell everyone the good news," He told her.

This SHEro told everyone, near and far, that Jesus had been raised from the dead, and how He'd healed her from years of sickness. Mary was the first to see Jesus alive, the first to hear His voice, and the first to tell others. What an amazing honor and responsibility!

Devotion

1. Before Jesus healed Mary, she had a lot of bad thoughts. Are there bad thoughts that come into your mind sometimes? Take a minute and ask Jesus to protect your mind from those bad thoughts and ask Him to give you good thoughts instead.

2. Mary was rejected by many people in her town. Have you ever felt left out by friends or family? Talk to God and tell Him how you feel and ask Him to show you His love for you.

3. Mary was the first to tell the disciples that Jesus was alive. Is there a friend in your life who does not know Jesus yet? How can you share Jesus with them?

SALOME: MOTHER OF JAMES AND JOHN

SHERo of the Gospels

"Some women were there, watching from a distance, including...
Salome. They had been followers of Jesus and had cared for him while
he was in Galilee."

Mark 15:40-41 (NLT)

Salome watched as her two grown sons disappeared down the dusty path from her home. It was getting dark and, as usual, James and John were headed to work for their father's fishing business. Nighttime was the best time to catch fish because the air was cool and the water quiet. Salome's husband, Zebedee, was already on his boat, getting ready to set sail.

As Salome watched her boys head off, she was reminded of when they were young and scared of the dark. As children, they would crawl into her bed at night and she would tell them her favorite stories from the Scriptures. They loved hearing how David battled Goliath and how Moses parted the Red Sea. But their favorite stories were about a coming King who would save Israel from all their enemies. She taught them that God was greater than any fear they would ever face.

As James and John grew, so did their faith that God would send a hero to rescue them. As children, they imagined they were warriors on a quest to search for a hidden King. However, as men, they no longer had time for such grand quests. They had work to do.

On this day, James and John fished all night and still did not catch any fish. They were so frustrated! The sun began to rise above the cool water of the Sea of Galilee. Exhausted from a long night, the brothers were cleaning their nets when a man approached their friend, Peter, whose boat was right next to theirs. "May I stand on your boat to teach the crowd?" He asked.

The fishermen had not noticed all the people on the shore! *This must be Jesus*, the brothers thought. They had been hearing about this simple man from Nazareth who was attracting so much attention with His teachings. They looked at each other with amazement.

Soon, Salome came to the harbor, just as she did every day. She loved to bring Zebedee and her sons breakfast after their long night of fishing. When she arrived, she saw the crowd gathered. *What is that stranger doing on Peter's boat?* she thought. Salome had known Peter since he was a child, and now he was a grown man with a family and fishing business of his own.

Salome leaned in and whispered to a woman at the back of the crowd, "What's going on? Who is this man?"

The woman replied, "It's Jesus—the one everyone has been talking about! Maybe He is the King we have all been waiting for!"

Quickly, Salome moved through the crowd. As she came nearer, she saw that Jesus was teaching right next to Zebedee, James, and John. They had a front row seat!

Salome looked at Jesus. She could tell there was something special about Him. Could Jesus be the mysterious King she had taught her boys about years ago?

When Jesus had finished speaking to the crowd, He turned to Peter and said, "Take your boat out a little farther and drop your nets into the water. Get ready; you are about to catch a lot of fish!"

All eyes were on Jesus. Everyone stayed close to shore, wanting to see what would happen next. Peter let down his nets into the deep waters, but when he tried to bring them back up, they were too heavy to lift! They were filled with fish! The crowd gasped.

Salome's mouth dropped open in shock. It was clear that God's power was in Jesus. From that moment forward, Salome and her boys never left His side for three whole years.

At first, Salome wondered what she could possibly give to Jesus and His friends who had left everything to follow Him. But she soon discovered that the greatest gift she could give was her motherly love. She enjoyed taking care of Jesus and His followers. If they were hungry, this SHEro prepared food. If they were tired, she found them a place to sleep. She spent her own money to make sure they had everything they needed.

One afternoon, as they were traveling down a dirt road, Salome kneeled before Jesus to ask Him a favor. Like most moms, she wanted the very best for her boys. She said to Him, "Can my sons have the honor of sitting next to you in your King- dom?"

Jesus looked into her eyes and said, "Oh, Salome, you do not know what you are asking. I will experience a great amount of suffering. Are they prepared to suffer, too?"

James and John overheard the conversation and said, "Yes, Jesus, we are!" Salome was proud that her boys would be will- ing to give up all they had to follow Jesus. But Jesus knew that the future would be difficult for James and John, and that they truly would give everything, even their lives.

Later, when Jesus was arrested by Roman soldiers, Salome was there. She wept as she watched Him carry the wooden cross He would soon be nailed to. Three days after Jesus died on the cross, Salome was with the women who discovered that Jesus' body was no longer in its grave. In fact, when they went to the tomb, they were greeted by angels!

"I know you are looking for Jesus," said one of the angels, "but I have good news. He is not here. He is alive! Go and tell everyone that even death could not defeat Him."

Salome dropped her things and ran as fast as she could. She could not wait to tell her boys. But suddenly, Jesus appeared in front of her! She cried tears of joy and relief. It had only been three days, but it felt like three years. It was so good to see Him!

As Salome held Jesus' hand, she was reminded of their conversation a couple of years earlier where she had asked Him if her sons could sit next to Him in His Kingdom. It was on that same road they were on now that He had said He would suffer greatly, and that had certainly come true. Then, she remembered what her boys had said. They had said they were also willing to suffer for Jesus.

The truth that Salome taught James and John—that God's love was greater than any fear—came true in both of their lives. Years later, James laid down his life in order for others to know the love of Jesus. John, filled with God's Spirit, wrote five books of the Bible and spent the last years of his life in prison and in exile on a remote island, because of his faith in Jesus. James and John learned that God's Kingdom looked different than they thought it would. His Kingdom is in our hearts and minds, through God's Holy Spirit.

Salome was a blessing to her boys, to Jesus, and to all of His friends because she selflessly offered her time, her love, and all she had. This mother's faithfulness changed the world and she will forever be remembered as a SHEro.

Devotion

1. At first, Salome felt like she did not have anything special to show Jesus how much she loved Him. She soon realized that her gift of motherly love could bless a lot of people. What is something you are good at that God can use to bless the people around you?

2. Salome wanted to be close to Jesus forever. What are some ways that you feel close to Jesus? (Here are some ideas: worship, prayer, being in nature, being creative or spending time with friends at church, etc.)

3. Salome and her sons expected God's Kingdom to look different than it did on Earth. His Kingdom is in our hearts and minds and comes to life through the way we live. How can you share the Kingdom of God in your community and in the world?

JOANNA

SHERo of Luke and Romans

"... Jesus traveled about from one town and village to another, proclaiming the good news of the kingdom of God. The Twelve were with Him, and also some women who had been cured of evil spirits and diseases: ... Joanna the wife of Chuza, the manager of Herod's household ... and many others. These women were helping to support them out of their own means."

Luke 8:1-3 (NIV)

King Herod, the ruler of Galilee, lived in a big and beautiful palace in the city of Tiberius on the shore of the Sea of Galilee. The walls were made from marble stones, and there were so many rooms that more than one hundred guests could stay at the same time! Each room was decorated with items made from real silver and gold.

Groves of lush, green trees filled the walkways and large statues lined the courtyards.

Many people lived with King Herod in his palace. One of these was a woman named Joanna. Her husband worked closely with the King, and Joanna was very respected in Herod's palace. She was kind to her servants and compassionate to everyone she encountered. Night and day, food filled their tables. Grapes, figs, and delicious meats sat on top of gold platters. Joanna was always dressed in the finest colorful silk.

But, though she had all she could ever want, Joanna was sick. She had been sick for years. Her body was weak, but no doctor could help her. They had tried them all!

Within the palace, deep in the basement, was a prison. This prison held many people who had fought against the government, but it also held a man named John the Baptist. He had been imprisoned for speaking about the coming Savior of Israel, Jesus. Daily, he was heard throughout the prison halls, shouting that he had seen the Savior of Israel with his own eyes. The guards tried to quiet him, but he would only yell louder. He would not be silent.

Joanna often heard John as she passed by the door that led to the basement. The more she heard, the more her curiosity grew. Could he be talking about the man Jesus, about whom Joanna had heard so many rumors?

Who was this Jesus? Could He heal her like He had healed so many others? Joanna had to see Him for herself. Maybe, if she left the palace, someone could tell her where to find Him.

Though weak and tired, she managed to wrap a silk scarf around her head and shoulders and slowly made her way to the palace horse stable. There, she climbed on top of her horse, stroked his sleek mane, and took off.

As she rode past the palace gates, she saw poverty everywhere. Beggars lined the streets, pleading for food and money. Her heart broke for those who lived without the comforts she enjoyed every day in Herod's palace.

She traveled to the shore of the Sea of Galilee and saw a huge crowd gathered around a man who was teaching them. *This must be Jesus!* In her heart, she knew it was Him. She made her way through the crowd, finding any open space to move closer to Jesus. Soon, she found herself next to Him. He had the kindest eyes Joanna had ever seen. She reached toward Jesus and managed to touch the edge of his robe.

Immediately, Joanna felt warm and tingly as Jesus' power touched her body. Soon, she felt her energy and strength returning. She was healed! Joanna had been sick for so long and no doctor had been able to help her, but with one touch, Jesus had made her well! Surely, He must be the Savior!

From that moment forward, Joanna became one of Jesus' disciples. No palace could compare to the beauty she found in Jesus. She would willingly give it up, to be near Jesus. She had always had compassion for the broken, but now she lived among them, with Jesus, and helped provide for their needs.

This SHERo was near Jesus until the day He died. She watched Him heal people and change their lives. She watched Him teach and pray with His friends. And, she watched as He took His last breath on the cross.

Three days later, she and some other women went to visit His tomb, and found it empty. Suddenly, two angels appeared to them and Joanna and her friends fell to the floor. They knew they were in the presence of God's messengers. The angels told the women that Jesus was alive! Joanna ran back to town with excitement and joy, and told the other disciples, "Jesus has risen!" Then, she went and shared the news at the palace. Many believed that Jesus was alive because of her.

When Jesus went back to Heaven after appearing to His friends and many other people, Joanna knew she could not go back to living in the comforts of Herod's palace. She longed to return to the needy and hurting people she had met during her time following Jesus. So, she became a missionary with her husband, telling everyone she encountered about how Jesus had changed their lives.

Many scholars think that Joanna is the same person as Junia, mentioned in Paul's letter to the Romans (Romans 16:7). "Joanna" is her Hebrew name and "Junia" is her Greek name. Paul called Junia an "apostle" who shared the good news of Jesus far and wide. This SHERo was imprisoned with Paul and eventually gave her life so all would know the man who had healed her and set her free. Giving up the comforts of this world, Joanna chose to live among the poor instead. For her sacrifice, she gained Heaven, where she will be close to Jesus forever.

Devotion

1. Joanna grew a love for the poor in her community. What are some ways you can help the poor in your community? (Some examples could be: drawing pictures for them, writing an encouraging note, collecting items of food or clothing to give away, etc.)

2. Joanna had been sick for years and she experienced a miracle healing through Jesus. Do you or someone you love need healing? If so, take a moment to ask God for a miraculous healing.

3. Joanna left the comforts and riches of Herod's palace to live among the poor. She traveled to other countries to share the love of Jesus and to take care of the poor. She was a missionary. Have you ever thought about being a missionary where you live or going to another country to share Jesus, like Joanna?

Tabitha

SHEro of Acts, Chapter 9

"There was a believer in Joppa named Tabitha. She was always doing kind things for others and helping the poor."

Acts 9:36 (NLT)

The seaport city of Joppa, in Israel, was a busy place. Ships were always coming and going, with merchants busily unloading their cargo to sell in the markets.

Often, in active cities like this one, the poor and hurting people are overlooked. But in Joppa, there was a home that shone brightly. It was known to all as a place of safety, even in the darkest times. This home belonged to a kind and generous woman named Tabitha.

A warm fire glowed, lighting the room where Tabitha sat with a group of women. These friends often spent their evenings together, sharing both the happy and the painful parts of their lives.

Tabitha was known for the way she loved all people, no matter who they were or where they came from. She gave of her time and resources generously because she was so grateful for how much God had given her. She had become a follower of Jesus, and received His Holy Spirit to live with her forever. From that day forward, her love for God grew and overflowed to the city around her.

Women both near and far found comfort in Tabitha's warm hugs and listening ear. She grieved with them in hard times and celebrated with them in happy times. She opened her home to anyone who needed a warm meal or the company of a friend.

Many of the women who came to Tabitha for help were widows—women whose husbands had died—and they were left alone to take care of their home and property. In those days, people took advantage of widows and tried to steal their homes and land. They were often left homeless with no way to pay for food or clothing.

Tabitha's love for these women made her take action. She was an excellent seamstress, and she realized she could use her gift of sewing to help women feel beautiful and valuable—something many of them had not felt for a long time. The women loved their pretty new dresses and proudly wore them for all to see. Word spread far and wide about the kindness and generosity of this woman in Joppa.

One day, Tabitha got very sick. As she lay in her bed, the same women she had taken care of were now taking care of her. They dipped strips of cloth into a bowl of cool water and laid them on her body as she shook with a fever. Tabitha's breaths were slow and shallow as she lay in her bed, very weak. Her friends prayed that her energy and cheerful spirit would soon return.

But as they waited, their hope faded, and the women watched as their SHERo took her last breath. Their hearts broke as they realized their helper, defender, and friend was now gone.

Suddenly, a man burst into the house. He told the women that Peter, one of Jesus' close friends, was visiting a nearby village. Just like Jesus, when Peter prayed for people, they were healed—some were even raised from the dead! Hope began to rise in the women's hearts.

"Please, go find Peter and ask him to come pray for Tabitha!" the women begged the man. They knew the Holy Spirit lived within Peter. They were hoping for a miracle.

The man ran as fast as he could to the nearby town of Lydda to find Peter. When he finally found him, he pleaded with him to come and pray for Tabitha.

Peter agreed, and they quickly returned to Joppa, bringing Peter straight to Tabitha's house. Many women surrounded her, crying loudly and praying to God with great sadness. As soon as they saw Peter, they begged him to pray for Tabitha and proudly held up the clothing she had made for them. It was evident to Peter that every piece had been made with care and compassion.

He placed his finger over his lips to quiet the women and politely asked for a moment alone with Tabitha's body. Peter kneeled down and gently took her hand in his. He remembered the way he had felt when Jesus died—he had thought all hope was lost! But when Jesus was raised from the dead by the power of the Holy Spirit, he had felt more joy than he had ever known. Peter wanted Tabitha's friends to feel the same joy he had felt.

Peter, filled with faith, said, "Tabitha, get up." Instantly, she opened her eyes, smiled, and sat up! Tabitha was alive! Happily, Peter took her by the hand and helped her to her feet. Then He called the women back into the room. They could not believe their eyes! The women shrieked and laughed with delight and hugged Tabitha so tightly that she squealed. Everyone thanked God for bringing her back to them. They were so excited!

News spread like wildfire that Tabitha was alive. Joppa was filled with celebration and many believed in Jesus for the first time. This SHERo continued to love her community, and spent the rest of her life caring for the poor and widows. Filled with the love of the Holy Spirit, Tabitha will forever be known as a woman who loved generously.

Devotion

1. Tabitha had a special place in her heart for the poor. She made the women beautiful dresses, which helped them feel valuable and loved. What is a way that you can help others feel special?

2. Is there something your family has that you could share or give to someone in need?

3. Tabitha was known for her kindness and generosity to all she met. How can you show kindness or generosity to those in your neighborhood or school?

LYDIA

SHERO of Acts, Chapter 16

"One of those listening was a woman from the city of Thyatira named Lydia, a dealer in purple cloth. She was a worshiper of God."

Acts 16:14 (NIV)

L ydia loved the sounds of the water's current, flowing over the stones along the river's bottom. She sat on a patch of grass along the riverbank, outside the gates of Philippi, a Roman colony in Greece. It was her favorite place to find peace. Here, in this very spot, she could feel God's presence stronger than anywhere else. She would close her eyes and all of her troubles would fade away as peace filled her spirit.

When she was twelve, Lydia's father had taken her from their home in Thyatira to see the Mediterranean Sea for the first time. She had never seen such a huge body of water! She fell in love with the sparkling blue water and the crashing waves. It was there, on the seashore, that she first discovered the special sea snails. These snails were known for producing purple "ink" that could be used as dye.

Lydia picked up as many snails as she could carry and figured out how to use their ink to dye her clothes purple—the color of royalty! She found tree branches and made them into a crown. "I am the Queen of the Mediterranean; you will do as I command," she yelled to the thundering waves. It was fun to pretend.

The snails were a wonderful find, as their ink was used all over the world to color fine cloth for expensive clothing. Young Lydia started her own business, making and selling purple dye and fabrics in markets throughout the region. One popular market was in Philippi, where she eventually made her home and discovered her peaceful river escape.

Although Lydia enjoyed her time alone with God, today she was expecting a group of women to join her at the river. These women met often to learn about the Scriptures. None of these women had ever heard about Jesus, but they loved God and looked forward to the time God would send a Savior to come save them.

Lydia was leading the group when two men approached. Their names were Paul and Silas, and they were followers of Jesus. They had heard what the women were talking about and began to share about the promised Savior the Scriptures talked about! They told the women about Jesus—how He had lived, died, and risen from the dead. He was the Rescuer they'd been waiting for!

Lydia was captivated by this news. She could feel God's presence as Paul and Silas spoke. She knew in her heart that what they were saying about Jesus was true.

"How do I follow Jesus?" she asked.

Paul told her, "Believe in your heart and declare out loud that Jesus is Lord! God's Holy Spirit will fill your heart and He will guide you." As they prayed together, God's love and joy filled Lydia and the same peace she always felt at the riverbank was now inside of her.

Lydia wanted even more. "What do I do now?" she asked. Paul pointed to the river behind her. He said she could be baptized to show she was now a follower of Jesus. (When we are baptized, we are lowered into the water, just as Jesus died and was lowered into the grave. As we are raised up from the water, we are raised into new life just as Jesus was raised from the dead.)

Right away, Lydia knew she wanted to do it. As Lydia was baptized in the river, she knew it was not just her body being cleaned, but her heart, too. She felt wonderful!

Lydia invited Paul and Silas to stay in her home as guests, so they could teach her and her family more about Jesus. This was a very bold thing for her to ask because, at this time, many people in Philippi did not like what these men taught. Philippi was known for worshipping false gods—even the Roman Emperor. But God's love was greater than her fear.

Paul and Silas agreed to stay, and many people in the city became followers of Jesus. Her home became a church—a place for Christians to gather and worship together. These new Christians came to Lydia's home from all over Philippi to learn more about God and how to follow Him.

Lydia still ran her purple dye business, and the money she made was used to help this group of Jesus' followers. The church in Lydia's home fed and clothed people in need while sharing God's gift of love.

However, some people were not excited about this new church. One day, when Paul and Silas were in Philippi, they were arrested and beaten for teaching about Jesus. When they were released, although their bodies were bruised and tired, they went and saw Lydia. She cried and thanked God that they were safe as she held her friends tightly, welcomed them in, and helped care for them.

Paul and Silas stayed with Lydia for a while and continued teaching the new believers from the Scriptures, and training leaders to run the church. They encouraged them to continue to teach the good news of Jesus, even though it was dangerous.

Lydia will forever be remembered for her courage, generosity, and leadership. This SHEro's courage started a church that led many people to Jesus—even when city leaders tried to stop them. Her generosity provided for the needs of others, and her leadership kept the church strong when Paul and Silas were arrested. Because of Lydia, the church in Philippi continued to grow. Philippi became known throughout the Roman empire for more than its purple dye. It was known as a city where people could experience the love of Jesus.

Devotion

1. Lydia was a businesswoman who loved to sell purple dye and cloth. She was passionate about purple from childhood. Is there anything that you are passionate about?

2. Do you think you will use your passions as a business when you get older? What might that look like (can you imagine)?

3. How can you give of your resources (time, money, skills, talents, etc.) to churches, Missionaries, or other organizations who show Jesus' love to the world?

PRISCILLA

SHERo of Acts and Romans

"Greet Priscilla and Aquila, my co-workers in Christ Jesus. They risked their lives for me. Not only I but all the churches of the Gentiles are grateful to them."

Romans 16:3-4 (NIV)

It was a clear night, and the stars and moon were shining brightly. As the fire was slowly going out, Priscilla looked lovingly at her husband, Aquila, who had fallen asleep after a long day's work. Priscilla looked up into the night sky and thought about how big God was and how He had always taken care of them, no matter what they faced.

Priscilla and Aquila were tentmakers who worked together to produce the finest custom tents in all of Corinth. They spent many hours crafting beautiful tent panels made of tightly woven goats' hair. Over time, these panels would bleach from exposure to the sun and need to be replaced. Priscilla and Aquila not only made the panels—they repaired them. They were good at it, and they stayed very busy.

Tentmaking was an important job in the Roman empire. Without tents, soldiers would have no protection from the sun or rain. Townspeople also used tents when they traveled to visit family or sell goods. Priscilla and Aquila's tents provided both shelter and safety for all who gathered inside them.

While living in Rome, they had heard about Jesus from someone teaching on the street. As they listened, both Priscilla and Aquila could feel God's Spirit speaking to their hearts. They began to pray and felt God's love fill them. Many others also responded to the teacher's message, and a new church was formed in Rome.

Priscilla was hungry to know more about Jesus. She studied the Scriptures with other new believers and her love for Jesus became the center of her life.

After some time, the Roman Emperor became angry with the Jewish people and kicked them out of Rome. Priscilla was sad to leave, but she knew God was with her and leading her on a new adventure. She felt confident God wanted to use her to do His work in a new city.

God led Priscilla and Aquila to the Greek city of Corinth, where they made their new home. Shortly after they were settled, they found a market and set up their tentmaking shop.

While they were selling their tents, a man named Paul— who also was a tentmaker—asked them if they had any work for him to do. They quickly became friends and realized that Paul was also a follower of Jesus! Not only that, but he was also an apostle—one who was sent out to tell the world about the good news of Jesus.

Paul needed a place to live, so Priscilla and Aquila invited him to stay with them in their home. They would talk late into the night, asking Paul questions about all he had seen God do. Priscilla loved to hear about Paul's adventures and how he helped start new churches on his journeys.

Soon, Priscilla's home became a church for all the new believers to meet in. They prayed, sang songs, and encouraged each other to grow in their faith, even when it was hard.

Being open about their Christian faith was dangerous for Priscilla and Aquila. In Corinth, many people hated these new Christians. But God said, "Do not be afraid to keep speaking! Do not be silent! For I am with you, and no one will hurt you because I have many people in this city who believe in me." This encouraged Priscilla, Aquila, and all the believers in Corinth to continue to share the good news of Jesus. Daily, more and more people chose to follow Jesus and joined the church family that met in their home.

After a year and a half, Priscilla, Aquila, and Paul traveled together to Ephesus to start another church. God's word was spreading everywhere! But soon, Paul left to continue God's work elsewhere and Priscilla and Aquila remained in Ephesus. Priscilla began to grow lonely, so she decided to meet people through her tentmaking business!

Priscilla loved to talk about Jesus with anyone who came to her stand at the market. She could not help but share how Jesus had changed her life! One day, she met a well-known preacher named Apollos. He was an amazing speaker. Priscilla invited him to stay with them in their home and shared all she and Aquila had learned about the power of the Holy Spirit. After this, Apollos preached with more power and even more people began to believe in Jesus. Because of Priscilla's boldness, once again, her home became a church for the new believers in Ephesus.

These were such wonderful memories of God's goodness. She loved to look back on her adventures. Sitting by the fire, Priscilla thanked God for always taking care of her. As she gazed at the stars, she was reminded of God's promise to fill the earth with children of God—more than all the stars in the night sky. Priscilla's boldness and bravery as a leader brought many people into the family of God, and she will forever be remembered as a SHEro.

Devotion

1. Priscilla loved to talk to everyone she met about her love for Jesus. No matter where she worked or lived, she shared her faith. How can you share your faith with family and friends?
2. Priscilla and her husband, Aquila, were a great team. Is there a friend in your life with whom you can partner to do acts of kindness at your school, community, or neighborhood?

*****

You have learned about many SHEROES in this book. Do you want to be one of God's SHEROES too? If your answer is, "Yes," then let's pray…

"God, I believe in You. I believe that You sent Your son Jesus to die for me because You love me so much. Thank You that Jesus rose from the dead and that He speaks to me today! Help me hear You when You talk to me. Help me be brave when You ask me to do something. Help me have eyes to see those who need help. Help me trust You and know You more every day. Jesus, I want to be Your SHERO! Amen."

"And now, O LORD God, I am your servant; do as you have promised…"

2 Samuel 7:25 (NLT)

ABOUT THE AUTHOR

as God ever spoken something over your life that you thought there was NO WAY it would ever come to pass? This book, *SHEROES of the Bible*, is a testament to God doing what He said He would do.

This book is very personal for me. Sadly, like many children, I was abused as a young child and lived, from that point forward, bound by fear. It was not until I learned that the Lord's love is stronger than fear that I found breakthrough. My breakthrough came through the stories of the men and women in the Bible who experienced God's love and freedom in the midst of their difficulties. I want everyone—young and old—to know that God can bring redemption and healing to the deepest parts of their hearts, where shame or regret dwell. His love changes everything!

Seven years ago, I was overwhelmed with raising two young kids and was dealing with crippling anxiety. One night, at my lowest point, my husband said to me, "Let's pray and see what God wants to say to you." I closed my eyes (reluctantly) and quietly waited... I heard nothing. But suddenly my husband said, "God is calling you an 'Author.' He says you're going to write books." I felt like Sarah, in the Bible, who was ninety years old when God told her she would get pregnant! I wanted to laugh— and not with joy, but with disbelief. All I could see was my anxiety and fear. But, praise God, He was bigger than my doubt! In His mercy, His will came to pass. He brought me out of that darkness for His divine purpose.

For anyone who may be feeling stuck and in need of a breakthrough, I want you to know that we are all on an adventure with the Lord. Sometimes parts of our story are dark and depressing, but the Lord promises to bring hope to every heart that looks to Him for breakthrough. He writes our story and He always gets the victory, no matter how dark, scary, or difficult the journey is. God is in control. He always wins!

Lauren

A free ebook edition is available with the purchase of this book.

To claim your free ebook edition:

1. Visit MorganJamesBOGO.com
2. Sign your name CLEARLY in the space
3. Complete the form and submit a photo of the entire copyright page
4. You or your friend can download the ebook to your preferred device

Morgan James
BOGO™

A **FREE** ebook edition is available for you
or a friend with the purchase of this print book.

CLEARLY SIGN YOUR NAME ABOVE

Instructions to claim your free ebook edition:
1. Visit MorganJamesBOGO.com
2. Sign your name CLEARLY in the space above
3. Complete the form and submit a photo
   of this entire page
4. You or your friend can download the ebook
   to your preferred device

Print & Digital Together Forever.

Snap a photo

Free ebook

Read anywhere

CPSIA information can be obtained
at www.ICGtesting.com
Printed in the USA
JSHW040347091121
20306JS00009B/16